UNTAMED YOUTH!

THE ULTIMATE VISUAL GUIDE

TO 50s & 60s ROCK & POP

AT THE MOVIES

Peter Checksfield

FOR HEATHER

ACKNOWLEDGEMENTS

This book wouldn't have been possible without the help of a great many film and music historians over the years. These include, but are certainly not limited to, James Ross, Tom Sturt, Gordon Irwin, Jock Barnson, Bobby Baity, Keith Badman, Gary Quinn, Dick Stoll, Gary Belich, Alex Radov, Ron Pierce and Riny Bade.

CONTENTS

v

p. 151 - The Gamblers / Marvin Gaye / The Gentrys / Gerry & The Pacemakers / The Lorne Gibson Trio / Wayne Gibson with The Dynamic Sounds / Astrud Gilberto & Stan Getz / The Goofers / Rosco Gordon & The Red Tops / Lesley Gore / Charlie Gracie / Lee Grant & The Capitols / The Grateful Dead / Dobie Gray / Johnny B. Great / Jimmy Griffin / Arlo Guthrie

p. 162 - Bill Haley & His Comets / Arch Hall, Jr / Roy Hamilton / Russ Hamilton / Sophie Hardy / Judy Harriet / Jet Harris / Jet Harris & Tony Meehan / Wee Willie Harris / Richie Havens / Nora Hayes / Heinz / Jimi Hendrix / Herman's Hermits / Colin Hicks / The Hollies / The Hondells / The Honeycombs / David Houston / Chris Howard & The Third World

p. 180 - Frank Ifield

p. 180 - Jackie & Gayle / Jackie & The Raindrops / Mick Jagger / Jan & Dean / Jan & Kelly / Jay & The Americans / The Jefferson Airplane / Marv Johnson / Paul Jones / Janis Joplin

p. 189 - Katch 22 / Suzie Kaye / The Terry Kennedy Group / Kenny & The Wranglers / The King Brothers / The Knickerbockers / Buddy Knox / Billy J. Kramer with The Dakotas

p. 193 - The LaDell Sisters / The Ladybirds / Don Lang & His Frantic Five / Julius LaRosa / Jack Larson / Caroline Lee & Judy Jason / John Lennon / Ketty Lester / Gary Lewis & The Playboys / Jerry Lee Lewis / John Leyton / Abbey Lincoln / The Litter / Little Richard / Julie London / The Long & The Short / Donna Loren / Los Bravos / The Lovin' Spoonful / Lulu / Bob Luman / Frankie Lymon & The Teenagers / Louis Lymon & The Teenchords / Kenny Lynch

p. 216 - The M6 / Gene McDaniels / Clyde McPhatter / Cindy Malone / The Mamas & The Papas / Jayne Mansfield / The Marcels / Ann-Margret / Wink Martindale / Toni Martinez / Glen Mason / Susan Maughan / The Mello-Kings / The Merseybeats / The Migil Five / Ken Miller / Roger Miller / The Mindbenders / The Miracles / Mary Ann Mosley / Moby Grape / The Modern Folk Quartet / The Mojos / The Monkees / The Moonglows / Patricia Morrow / Jennifer Moss / Billy Myles

p. 238 - The Nashville Teens / Rick Nelson / Sandy Nelson / Anthony Newley / The Niteshades / Patsy Ann Noble / The Nooney Rickett Four

p. 245 - Quinn O'Hara / Johnny Olenn / Roy Orbison / The Orchids / Johnny Otis / The Outlaws

p. 248 - The Paris Sisters / Carl Perkins / Peter & Gordon / Peter, Paul & Mary / Pink Floyd / The Platters / Brian Poole & The Tremeloes / Preacher Smith & The Deacons / Elvis Presley / Mike Preston / The Pretty Things / Piccola Pupa / The Pyramids

p. 275 - Tommy Quickly & The Remo Four / The Quicksilver Messenger Service

Peter Checksfield

INTRODUCTION

There have been several books on Rock and Pop Movies, but these are usually more about the movies than the music, ie. The Director, the actors and the storylines. With a handful of notable exceptions, few of these movies could ever be described as great works of art, but many collectors seek them out purely for the musical performances.

Following several acclaimed but very wordy books on music and TV, I decided on a very different approach. The list of artists, movies and songs performed are all there, but rather than go for in-depth reviews, I've instead featured screenshots - over 700 of them!

Almost every movie mentioned in this book is available to view, either via official DVDs, circulating bootlegs or YouTube. However, in my research there are three that I've been unable to track down, or even find a trailer for: these are 'Hawaiian Boy' (1959), 'Farewell Performance' (1963) and 'Africa Shakes' (1966). In all these cases I used surviving on-set photos or posters to illustrate the artists' performances.

I have NOT included movies where artists just contribute to the soundtrack without appearing in person (no 'The Graduate' or 'Easy Rider'), nor have I included movies where the artist only attempts to act, without performing any songs (such as 'The Girl On A Motorcycle' and 'Work Is A Four-Letter Word'). Also not included are later retrospective documentaries.

I hope you enjoy what is, in my biased opinion, the ultimate visual guide to 50s & 60s music at the Movies!

Peter Checksfield

JULIA AMBER

SWEET BEAT (1959)

[USA: THE AMOROUS SEX]

UK - Black & White

Songs: Thanks / Recently / How Do You Mend A Broken Heart

AMEN CORNER

SCREAM AND SCREAM AGAIN (1969)

UK - Colour

Songs: Scream and Scream Again

THE ANIMALS

UK SWINGS AGAIN (1964)

UK - Colour

Songs: Baby Let Me Take You Home

GET YOURSELF A COLLEGE GIRL (1964)

[UK: THE SWINGING SET]

USA - Colour

Songs: Blue Feeling / Around and Around

POP GEAR (1965)

[USA: GO GO MANIA]

UK - Colour

Songs: House Of The Rising Sun / Don't Let Me Be Misunderstood

IT'S A BIKINI WORLD (1967)

USA - Colour

Songs: We Gotta Get Out Of This Place

MONTEREY POP (1968)

USA - Colour

Songs: Paint It Black [performed by Eric Burdon and The Animals]

NOTE: It's A Bikini World was filmed in 1965 and Monterey Pop was filmed in 1967.

PAUL ANKA

LET'S ROCK (1958)

[UK: KEEP IT COOL]

USA - Black & White

Songs: I'm Still Waiting Here For You

GIRL'S TOWN (1959)

USA - Black & White

Songs: Lonely Boy / Ave Maria / It's Time To Cry

REY ANTON

DATELINE DIAMONDS (1965)

UK - Black & White

Songs: First Taste Of Love

THE APPLEJACKS

UK SWINGS AGAIN (1964)

UK - Colour

Songs: Tell Me When / Like Dreamers Do

JUST FOR YOU (1964)

[USA: DISK-O-TEK HOLIDAY]

UK - Colour

Songs: Tell Me When

MAUREEN ARTHUR

HOT ROD GANG (1958)

[UK: FURY UNLEASHED]

USA - Black & White

Songs: Choo-choo Choo-boochie

JOHN ASHLEY

HOW TO MAKE A MONSTER (1958)

USA - Black & White

Songs: You've Got to Have Ee-Ooo

HOT ROD GANG (1958)

[UK: FURY UNLEASHED]

USA - Black & White

Songs: Hit and Run Lover / Believe Me / Annie Laurie

HOW TO STUFF A WILD BIKINI (1965)

USA - Colour

Songs: How to Stuff A Wild Bikini / That's What I Call A Healthy Girl

THE ASTRONAUTS

SURF PARTY (1964)

USA - Black & White

Songs: Fire Water / Surf Party

WILD ON THE BEACH (1965)

USA - Black & White

Songs: Rock This World / Little Speedy Gonzalez / Pyramid Stomp / Snap It

WILD WILD WINTER (1966)

USA - Colour

Songs: A Change Of Heart

OUT OF SIGHT (1966)

USA - Colour

Songs: Baby, Please Don't Go

FRANKIE AVALON

JAMBOREE! (1957)

[UK: DISC JOCKEY JAMBOREE]

USA - Black & White

Songs: I Don't Want To Be Teacher's Pet

OPERATION BIKINI (1963)

USA - Black & White

Songs: The Girl Back Home

BEACH PARTY (1963)

[UK: BEACH PARTY, U.S.A.]

USA - Colour

Songs: Beach Party / Don't Stop Now

MUSCLE BEACH PARTY (1964)

USA - Colour

Songs: Runnin' Wild / Surfer's Holiday [with Annette Funicello] / A Girl Needs A Boy (Part 2)

BIKINI BEACH (1964)

USA - Colour

Songs: Gimme Your Love, Yeah Yeah Yeah / How About That [with The Pyramids] / Because You're You [with Annette Funicello]

BEACH BLANKET BINGO (1965)

USA - Colour

Songs: Beach Blanket Bingo [with Annette Funicello] / I Think You Think [with Annette Funicello] / These Are the Good Times

SKI PARTY (1965)

USA - Colour

Songs: Ski Party / Lots, Lots More / Paintin' the Town [with Deborah Walley, Dwayne Hickman and Yvonne Craig]

HOW TO STUFF A WILD BIKINI (1965)

USA - Colour

Songs: If It's Gonna Happen [with Annette Funicello, Dwayne Hickman and Irene Tsu]

16

SERGEANT DEAD HEAD (1965)

USA - Colour

Songs: The Difference In Me Is You / Let's Play Love [with Deborah Walley]

FIREBALL 500 (1966)

USA - Colour

Songs: Fireball 500 / My Way / Turn Around / A Chance Like That / Country Carnival

Later Movies: Grease (1978)

THE BACHELORS

IT'S ALL OVER TOWN (1964)

UK - Colour

Songs: The Stars Will Remember

JUST FOR YOU (1964)

[USA: DISK-O-TEK HOLIDAY]

UK - Colour

Songs: The Fox / Low In The Valley

I'VE GOTTA HORSE (1965)

UK - Colour

Songs: Far Far Away / He's Got The Whole World In His Hands

JOAN BAEZ

THE BIG T.N.T. SHOW (1966)

USA - Black & White

Songs: 500 Miles / There But For Fortune / You've Lost That Lovin' Feeling

FESTIVAL (1967)

USA - Black & White

Songs: Go Tell Aunt Rhody [with Peter Yarrow] / Mary Hamilton / All My Trials / Colours [with Donovan] / Farewell Angelina

DONT LOOK BACK (1967)

USA - Black & White

Songs: Percy's Song / Love Is Just A Four-Letter Word / Sweeter Than The Flowers

WOODSTOCK (1970)

USA - Colour

Songs: Joe Hill / Swing Low Sweet Chariot

NOTE: The Big T.N.T. Show, Festival and Don't Look Back were filmed in 1965 and Woodstock was filmed in 1969.

<u>**LAVERN BAKER**</u>

ROCK ROCK ROCK! (1956)

USA - Black & White

Songs: Tra La La

MISTER ROCK AND ROLL! (1957)

USA - Black & White

Songs: Humpty Dumpty Heart / Love Me Right In The Morning

THE BAKER TWINS

EVERY DAY'S A HOLIDAY (1964)

[USA: SEASIDE SWINGERS]

UK - Colour

Songs: Romeo Jones

A BAND OF ANGELS

JUST FOR YOU (1964)

[USA: DISK-O-TEK HOLIDAY]

UK - Colour

Songs: Hide 'n' Seek

THE BARBARIANS

THE T.A.M.I. SHOW (1964)

[UK: TEEN AGE COMMAND PERFORMANCE]

USA - Black & White

Songs: Hey Little Bird

AMANDA BARRIE

I'VE GOTTA HORSE (1965)

UK - Colour

Songs: Men / You Gotta Look Right For The Part [with Billy Fury, Jon Pertwee and Michael Medwin] / Grand Finale Medley: I've Gotta Horse – I Like Animals – Find Your Dreams – I've Gotta Horse [with cast] / Wonderful Day [with cast]

THE JOHN BARRY SEVEN

SIX-FIVE SPECIAL (1958)

UK - Black & White

Songs: You've Gotta Way / Ev'ry Which Way

CURLY PAT BARRY

ROCK YOU SINNERS (1957)

UK - Black & White

Songs: Stop It (I Like It)

ART BAXTER AND HIS ROCKIN' SINNERS

ROCK YOU SINNERS (1957)

UK - Black & White

Songs: Dixieland Rock / Rock You Sinners / Art's Theme

THE BEACH BOYS

ONE MAN'S CHALLENGE (1962)

USA - Black & White

Songs: Surfin' Safari

THE MONKEY'S UNCLE (1964)

USA - Colour

Songs: The Monkey's Uncle [with Annette Funicello]

THE T.A.M.I. SHOW (1964)

[UK: TEEN AGE COMMAND PERFORMANCE]

USA - Black & White

Songs: Surfin' USA / I Get Around / Surfer Girl / Dance, Dance, Dance

THE GIRLS ON THE BEACH (1965)

USA - Colour

Songs: The Girls On The Beach / Lonely Sea / Little Honda

THE BEATLES

A HARD DAY'S NIGHT (1964)

UK - Black & White

Songs: A Hard Day's Night / I Should Have Known Better (version #1) / If I Fell (version #1) / Can't Buy Me Love / And I Love Her / I'm Happy Just To Dance With You / Tell Me Why / If I Fell (version #2) / I Should Have Known Better (version #2) / She Loves You

A HARD DAY'S NIGHT [OUTTAKE] (1964)

UK - Black & White

Songs: You Can't Do That

POP GEAR (1965)

[USA: GO GO MANIA]

UK - Colour

Songs: Twist and Shout / She Loves You

HELP! (1965)

UK - Colour

Songs: Help! / You're Going To Lose That Girl / You've Got To Hide Your Love Away / Ticket To Ride / I Need You / The Night Before / Another Girl

MAGICAL MYSTERY TOUR (1967)

UK - Colour

Songs: Magical Mystery Tour / The Fool On The Hill / Flying / I Am The Walrus / Blue Jay Way / Your Mother Should Know

YELLOW SUBMARINE (1968)

UK - Colour

Songs: Yellow Submarine / Eleanor Rigby / All Together Now (version #1) / When I'm 64 / Only A Northern Song / Nowhere Man / Lucy In The Sky With Diamonds / Sgt. Pepper's Lonely Hearts Club Band / With A Little Help From My Friends / All You Need Is Love / Hey Bulldog / It's All Too Much / All Together Now (version #2)

LET IT BE (1970)

UK - Colour

Songs: Adagio For Strings / Don't Let Me Down (version #1) / Maxwell's Silver Hammer / Two Of Us (version #1) / I've Got A Feeling (version #1) / Oh! Darling / One After 909 (version #1) / Piano Boogie / Across The Universe / Dig A Pony (version #1) / Suzy Parker / I Me Mine / For Your Blue / Besame Mucho / Octopus's Garden / You've Really Got A Hold Of Me / The Long and Winding Road (version #1) / Medley: Rip It Up - Shake Rattle and Roll / Medley: Kansas City - Miss Ann - Lawdy Miss Clawdy / Dig It / Two Of Us (version #2) / Let It Be / The Long and Winding Road (version #2) / Get Back (version #1) / Don't Let Me Down (version #2) / I've Got A Feeling (version #2) / One After 909 (version #2) / Dig A Pony (version #2) / Get Back (version #2) / Get Back (version #3, audio only over credits)

NOTE: The Beatles' songs in Pop Gear were filmed in Manchester in 1963.

THE BEAU BRUMMELS

VILLAGE OF THE GIANTS (1965)

USA - Colour

Songs: Woman / When It Comes To Your Love

WILD WILD WINTER (1966)

USA - Colour

Songs: Just Wait and See

THE BEE GEES

CUCUMBER CASTLE (1970)

Songs: Don't Forget To Remember / Then You Left Me / I Was The Child / The Lord / My Thing

NOTE: Cucumber Castle was filmed in 1969.

FREDDIE BELL AND THE BELLBOYS

ROCK AROUND THE CLOCK (1956)

USA - Black & White

Songs: Teach You To Rock / Giddy Up A Ding Dong

GET YOURSELF A COLLEGE GIRL (1964)

[UK: THE SWINGING SET]

USA - Colour

Songs: Talkin' About Love [with Roberta Linn]

THE BELEW TWINS

ROCK BABY - ROCK IT (1957)

USA - Black & White

Songs: Lonesome / Love Me Baby

DICKIE BENNETT

ROCK YOU SINNERS (1957)

UK - Black & White

Songs: Heartbreak Hotel / How Many Times? / Cry Upon My Shoulder

BROOK BENTON

MISTER ROCK AND ROLL! (1957)

USA - Black & White

Songs: If Only I Had Known

CHUCK BERRY

ROCK ROCK ROCK! (1956)

USA - Black & White

Songs: You Can't Catch Me

MISTER ROCK AND ROLL! (1957)

USA - Black & White

Songs: Oh Baby Doll

GO, JOHNNY, GO! (1959)

USA - Black & White

Songs: Johnny B. Goode / Memphis, Tennessee / Little Queenie

JAZZ ON A SUMMER'S DAY (1960)

USA - Colour

Songs: Sweet Little Sixteen

THE T.A.M.I. SHOW (1964)

[UK: TEEN AGE COMMAND PERFORMANCE]

USA - Black & White

Songs: Johnny B. Goode / Maybelline / Sweet Little Sixteen / Nadine

SWEET TORONTO (1971)

USA - Colour

Songs: Johnny B. Goode

NOTE: Sweet Toronto was filmed in 1969, and was reissued in extended form as 'Keep On Rockin'' in 1972, with a further additional song appearing in 'Alice In The Cities' in 1974.

Later Movies: Let The Good Times Roll (1973), The London Rock & Roll Show (1973), American Hot Wax (1978), National Lampoon's Class Reunion (1982), Hail! Hail! Rock 'n' Roll (1987)

DAVE BERRY

THE GHOST GOES GEAR (1966)

UK - Colour

Songs: Mama / Now

THE BIRDS

THE DEADLY BEES (1966)

UK - Colour

Songs: That's All I Need You For

BILL BLACK'S COMBO

TEENAGE MILLIONAIRE (1961)

USA - Black & White

Songs: Smokie, Part 2 / Yogi

CILLA BLACK

FERRY CROSS THE MERSEY (1964)

UK - Black & White

Songs: Is It Love

THE BLACK KNIGHTS

FERRY CROSS THE MERSEY (1964)

UK - Black & White

Songs: I Got A Woman

RORY BLACKWELL AND THE BLACKJACKS

ROCK YOU SINNERS (1957)

UK - Black & White

Songs: Intro To The Rock / Rockin' With Rory

THE BLACKWELLS

FERRY CROSS THE MERSEY (1964)

UK - Black & White

Songs: Why Don't You Love Me

JOYCE BLAIR

BE MY GUEST (1965)

UK - Black & White

Songs: Gotta Get Away Now

THE BLOCKBUSTERS

ROCK ALL NIGHT (1957)

USA - Black & White

Songs: Rock All Night / I Wanna Rock Now / Rock 'n' Roll Guitar

THE GRAHAM BOND ORGANISATION

GONKS GO BEAT (1965)

UK - Colour

Songs: Harmonica / Drum Battle

GARY U.S. BONDS

IT'S TRAD DAD! (1962)

[USA: RING-A-DING RHYTHM!]

UK - Black & White

Songs: Seven Day Weekend

THE BONZO DOG DOO-DAH BAND

MAGICAL MYSTERY TOUR (1967)

UK - Colour

Songs: Death Cab For Cutie

PAT BOONE

BERNADINE (1957)

USA - Colour

Songs: Bernadine / Technique / Love Letters In The Sand

APRIL LOVE (1957)

USA - Colour

Songs: Clover In The Meadow / Give Me A Gentle Girl / April Love / April Love (Reprise) [with Shirley Jones] / Do It Yourself [with Shirley Jones, Dolores Michaels and Bradford Jackson] / The Bentonville Fair [with Shirley Jones and cast] / April Love (Finale) [with Shirley Jones and cast]

MARDI GRAS (1958)

USA - Colour

Songs: Bourbon Street Blues / Loyalty [with Steve Allen] / Bigger Than Texas / A Fiddle, A Rifle, An Axe, and A Bible

ALL HANDS ON DECK (1961)

USA - Colour

Songs: All Hands On Deck / Somewhere There's Home / I've Got It Made / You Mean Everything To Me

STATE FAIR (1962)

USA - Colour

Songs: That's For Me / Willing and Eager [with Ann-Margret] / It's A Grand Night For Singing [with Ann-Margret and Bobby Darin]

THE MAIN ATTRACTION (1962)

USA - Colour

Songs: The Main Attraction / Gondoli, Gondola / Si, Si, Si / Amore Baciami

THE HORROR OF IT ALL (1964)

UK - Black & White

Songs: The Horror Of It All

JIMMY BOWEN

JAMBOREE! (1957)

[UK: DISC JOCKEY JAMBOREE]

USA - Black & White

Songs: Cross Over

DAVID BOWIE

LOVE YOU TILL TUESDAY (1969)

UK - Colour

Songs: Love You Till Tuesday / Sell Me A Coat / When I'm Five / Rubber Band / The Mask (a mime) / Let Me Sleep Beside You / Ching-A-Ling / Space Oddity / When I Live My Dream

THE BROOK BROTHERS

IT'S TRAD DAD! (1962)

[USA: RING-A-DING RHYTHM!]

UK - Black & White

Songs: Double Trouble

DONNIE BROOKS

A SWINGIN' SUMMER (1965)

USA - Colour

Songs: Pennie The Poo

ARTHUR BROWN

THE COMMITTEE (1968)

UK - Black & White

Songs: Nightmare

Later Movies: Glastonbury Fayre (1972), Tommy (1975)

BARBARA BROWN AND PERRY FORD

GONKS GO BEAT (1965)

UK - Colour

Songs: In Love With You Today [Perry Ford only] / Penny For Your Thoughts [Barbara Brown only] / Loving You / It Take Two To Make Love /

JAMES BROWN

THE T.A.M.I. SHOW (1964)

[UK: TEEN AGE COMMAND PERFORMANCE]

USA - Black & White

Songs: Out Of Sight / Prisoner Of Love / Please, Please, Please / Night Train

SKI PARTY (1965)

USA - Colour

Songs: I Got You (I Feel Good)

Later Movies: The Blues Brothers (1980)

JOE BROWN

WHAT A CRAZY WORLD (1963)

UK - Black & White

Songs: Bruvvers [with Grazina Frame and Michael Goodman] / Oh What A Family [with Marty Wilde] / Wasn't It A Handsome Punch-Up [with Marty Wilde] / Independence / I Feel The Same Way Too [with Susan Maughan] / Just You Wait and See / What A Crazy World We're Living In [with Marty Wilde and Susan Maughan]

JUST FOR FUN (1963)

UK - Black & White

Songs: Let Her Go / What's The Name Of The Game

THREE HATS FOR LISA (1965)

UK - Colour

Songs: This Is A Special Day / Something Tells Me (I Shouldn't Do This) [with Una Stubbs and Dave Nelson] / I'm The King Of The Castle [with Una Stubbs and Dave Nelson] / Bermondsey [with Sophie Hardy, Sid James, Una Stubbs and Dave Nelson] / L O N D O N (London Town) [with Sophie Hardy, Sid James, Una Stubbs and Dave Nelson] / Three Hats for Lisa [with Sophie Hardy, Sid James, Una Stubbs and Dave Nelson] / Two Cockney Kids [with Una Stubbs] / Have You Heard About Johnny Howjego [with Sid James, Una Stubbs and Dave Nelson] / That What Makes A Girl A Girl [with cast] / One Day in London [with cast]

GEORGE 'CALYPSO' BROWNE

ROCK YOU SINNERS (1957)

UK - Black & White

Songs: Rock 'n' Roll Calypso

CLIMB UP THE WALL (1960)

UK - Black & White

Songs: Frankie and Johnny

THE JOHNNY BURNETTE TRIO

ROCK ROCK ROCK! (1956)

USA - Black & White

Songs: Lonesome Train (On A Lonesome Track)

THE BYRDS

THE BIG T.N.T. SHOW (1966)

USA - Black & White

Songs: Turn! Turn! Turn! / The Bells Of Rhymney / Mr. Tambourine Man

NOTE: The Big T.N.T. Show was filmed in 1965.

SUSAN CABOT

CARNIVAL ROCK (1957)

USA - Black & White

Songs: Ou-Shoo-Bla-D / There's No Place Without You

THE CADILLACS

GO, JOHNNY, GO! (1959)

USA - Black & White

Songs: Jay Walker / Please, Mr. Johnson

JO ANN CAMPBELL

GO, JOHNNY, GO! (1959)

USA - Black & White

Songs: Mama, Can I Go Out

HEY, LET'S TWIST! (1961)

USA - Black & White

Songs: Shake Me Baby

CANNED HEAT

MONTEREY POP (1968)

USA - Colour

Songs: Rollin' and Tumblin'

WOODSTOCK (1970)

USA - Colour

Songs: A Change Is Gonna Come [Director's Cut only]

NOTE: Monterey Pop was filmed in 1967 and Woodstock was filmed 1969.

FREDDY CANNON

JUST FOR FUN (1963)

UK - Black & White

Songs: It's Been Nice (I Gotta Get Up Early In The Morning) / The Ups and Downs Of Love

VILLAGE OF THE GIANTS (1965)

USA - Colour

Songs: Little Bitty Corrine

DISK-O-TEK HOLIDAY (1966)

[UK alternate edit: JUST FOR YOU]

UK/US - Colour

Songs: Medley: Tallahassee Lassie - Abigail Beecher - Buzz Buzz A-Diddle-It / Beechwood City

JOHNNY CARROLL

ROCK BABY - ROCK IT (1957)

USA - Black & White

Songs: Crazy Crazy Lovin' / Wild Wild Women / Rockin' Maybel / Sugar Baby

THE CARROLL BROTHERS

DON'T KNOCK THE TWIST (1962)

USA - Black & White

Songs: Hey Bo Diddley

THE CASCADES

CATALINA CAPER (1967)

USA - Colour

Songs: There's A New World

THE CASTAWAYS

IT'S A BIKINI WORLD (1967)

USA - Colour

Songs: Liar, Liar

JOHNNY CASH

FIVE MINUTES TO LIVE (1961)

USA - Black & White

Songs: Five Minutes To Live

HOOTENANNY HOOT (1963)

USA - Black & White

Songs: Frankie's Man Johnny

FESTIVAL (1967)

USA - Black & White

Songs: I Walk The Line

NOTE: The Festival was filmed in 1964

JIMMY CAVALLO AND HIS HOUSE ROCKERS

ROCK ROCK ROCK! (1956)

USA - Black & White

Songs: Rock, Rock, Rock / The Big Beat

ANDY CAVELL AND THE SAINTS

LIVE IT UP! (1963)

[USA: SING AND SWING]

UK - Black & White

Songs: Don't Take You From Me

THE CELL BLOCK SEVEN

ROCK BABY - ROCK IT (1957)

USA - Black & White

Songs: Love Me Baby / When The Saints Go Marching In

GENE CHANDLER

DON'T KNOCK THE TWIST (1962)

USA - Black & White

Songs: Duke Of Earl

THE CHANTELLES

DATELINE DIAMONDS (1965)

UK - Black & White

Songs: I Think Of You / Please Don't Kiss Me

RAY CHARLES

SWINGIN' ALONG (1961)

USA - Colour

Songs: What'd I Say / Sticks and Stones

BALLAD IN BLUE (1964)

[USA: BLUES FOR LOVERS]

UK - Black & White

Songs: What'd I Say / Don't Tell Me Your Troubles / I Got A Woman / Light Out Of Darkness / That Lucky Old Sun / Careless Love / Talkin' 'Bout You / Busted / Let The Good Times Roll / Hit The Road Jack / Unchain My Heart / Hallelujah I Love Her So

THE BIG T.N.T. SHOW (1966)

USA - Black & White

Songs: What'd I Say / Georgia On My Mind / Let The Good Times Roll

NOTE: The Big T.N.T. Show was filmed in 1965.

Later Movies: The Blues Brothers (1980)

TOMMY CHARLES

SHAKE, RATTLE & ROCK! (1956)

USA - Black & White

Songs: Sweet Love On My Mind

CHUBBY CHECKER

TEENAGE MILLIONAIRE (1961)

USA - Black & White

Songs: The Jet / Let's Twist Again

TWIST AROUND THE CLOCK (1961)

USA - Black & White

Songs: Twistin' USA / Your Lips and Mine / Twist Along / Twist Around The Clock [with Clay Cole]

DON'T KNOCK THE TWIST (1962)

USA - Black & White

Songs: (We're Goin') Twistin' / La Paloma Twist / I Love To Twist / The Fly / Slow Twistin' [with Dee Dee Sharp] / Don't Knock The Twist

IT'S TRAD DAD! (1962)

[USA: RING-A-DING RHYTHM!]

UK - Black & White

Songs: Lose Your Inhibition Twist

<u>THE CHIFFONS</u>

DISK-O-TEK HOLIDAY (1966)

[UK alternate edit: JUST FOR YOU]

UK/US - Colour

Songs: Nobody Knows What's Going On (In My Mind)

THE CHOCOLATE WATCHBAND

RIOT ON SUNSET STRIP (1967)

USA - Colour

Songs: Don't Need Your Lovin'

THE LOVE-INS (1967)

USA - Colour

Songs: Are You Gonna Be There (At The Love-In)

JORDAN CHRISTOPHER

ANGEL, ANGEL, DOWN WE GO (1969)

USA - Colour

Songs: Angel, Angel, Down We Go

CIRINO AND THE BOWTIES

ROCK ROCK ROCK! (1956)

USA - Black & White

Songs: Rock, Pretty Baby [with Ivy Schulman] / Ever Since I Can Remember

JIMMY CLANTON

GO, JOHNNY, GO! (1959)

USA - Black & White

Songs: My Love Is Strong / It Takes A Long, Long Time / Ship On A Stormy Sea / Once Again [with Sandy Stewart]

TEENAGE MILLIONAIRE (1961)

USA - Black & White

Songs: Teenage Millionaire / Possibility / Green Light

THE DAVE CLARK FIVE

RAG DOLL (1961)

[USA: YOUNG, WILLING AND EAGER]

UK - Black & White

Songs: Instrumental / Why Am I Living [with Jess Conrad]

PIT OF DARKNESS (1961)

UK - Black & White

Songs: Various Instrumentals / My Heart Is The Lover [with Ronnie Hall]

GET YOURSELF A COLLEGE GIRL (1964)

[UK: THE SWINGING SET]

USA - Colour

Songs: Whenever You're Around / Thinking Of You Baby

CATCH US IF YOU CAN (1965)

[USA: HAVING A WILD WEEKEND]

UK - Black & White

Songs: Catch Us If You Can / Sweet Memories / Time / When / I Can't Stand It / On The Move / Move By / Ol Sol / Having A Wild Weekend

HITS IN ACTION (1968)

UK - Black & White

Songs: Try Too Hard / I Need Love / Come Home / Having A Wild Weekend + excerpts of other songs

NOTE: The two 1961 movies were filmed on the same set and on the same day! Much of Hits In Action was previously seen in a 1968 TV special entitled 'Hold On, It's The Dave Clark Five'.

PETULA CLARK

SIX-FIVE SPECIAL (1958)

UK - Black & White

Songs: Baby Lover

THE BIG T.N.T. SHOW (1966)

USA - Black & White

Songs: Downtown / You're The One / My Love

FINIAN'S RAINBOW (1968)

USA - Colour

Songs: Look To The Rainbow / How Are Things In Glocca Morra? [with Fred Astaire] / Old Devil Moon [with Don Francks] / Something Sort of Grandish [with Tommy Steele] / If This Isn't Love [with Don Francks and Fred Astaire] / That Great Come-And-Get-It Day [with Don Francks] / When The Idle Poor Become The Idle Rich [with Fred Astaire] / Old Devil Moon (reprise) [with Don Francks] / How Are Things in Glocca Morra? [with cast]

GOODBYE, MR. CHIPS (1969)

USA - Colour

Songs: Walk Through The World / Fill The World With Love / Medley: Entr'Acte - What Shall I Do With Today? / And The Sky Smiled / Schooldays / You and I

NOTE: The Big T.N.T. Show was filmed in 1965.

THE CLEAR LIGHT

THE PRESIDENT'S ANALYST (1967)

USA - Colour

Songs: She's Ready To Be Free

DON COATS AND THE BON-AIRES

ROCK BABY - ROCK IT (1957)

USA - Black & White

Songs: Stop The World / China Star / Love Never Forgets

EDDIE COCHRAN

THE GIRL CAN'T HELP IT (1956)

USA - Colour

Songs: Twenty Flight Rock

UNTAMED YOUTH (1957)

USA - Black & White

Songs: Cotton Picker

GO, JOHNNY, GO! (1959)

USA - Black & White

Songs: Teenage Heaven

JOE COCKER

WOODSTOCK (1970)

USA - Colour

Songs: With A Little Help From My Friends

NOTE: Woodstock was filmed in 1969.

THE COCKNEYS

SWINGING UK (1964)

UK - Colour

Songs: After Tomorrow

CLAY COLE

TWIST AROUND THE CLOCK (1961)

USA - Black & White

Songs: Twist Around The Clock / The Twist Is Here To Stay / Don't Twist With Anyone Else (But Me) / (I'm Over) Here, There and Everywhere

THE COMFORTABLE CHAIR

HOW TO COMMIT MARRIAGE (1969)

USA - Colour

Songs: Let Me Through

CAROL CONNORS

CATALINA CAPER (1967)

USA - Colour

Songs: Book Of Love

JESS CONRAD

RAG DOLL (1961)

[USA: YOUNG, WILLING AND EAGER]

UK - Black & White

Songs: Why Am I Living [with The Dave Clark Five]

THE QUEEN'S GUARDS (1961)

UK - Black & White

Songs: Oh Susannah

THE GOLDEN HEAD (1964)

UK - Black & White

Songs: The Golden Head / Things I'd Like To Say

LOUISE CORDET

JUST FOR FUN (1963)

UK - Black & White

Songs: Which Way The Wind Blows

JUST FOR YOU (1964)

[USA: DISK-O-TEK HOLIDAY]

UK - Colour

Songs: It's So Hard To Be Good

LYN CORNELL

JUST FOR FUN (1963)

UK - Black & White

Songs: Kisses Can Lie

COUNTRY JOE AND THE FISH

MONTEREY POP (1968)

USA - Colour

Songs: Section 43

REVOLUTION (1968)

USA - Colour

Songs: Feel-Like-I'm-Fixing-To-Die-Rag

WOODSTOCK (1970)

USA - Colour

Songs: Rock and Soul Music / Feel-Like-I'm-Fixing-To-Die-Rag

NOTE: Monterey Pop was filmed in 1967 and Woodstock was filmed in 1969.

JIMMY CRAWFORD

PLAY IT COOL (1962)

UK - Black & White

Songs: Take It Easy

CREAM

DET VAR EN LORDAG AFTEN (1968)

Denmark - Colour

Songs: World Of Pain / We're Going Wrong

THE CRICKETS

JUST FOR FUN (1963)

UK - Black & White

Songs: My Little Girl / Teardrops Fall Like Rain

THE GIRLS ON THE BEACH (1965)

USA - Colour

Songs: (They Call Her) La Bamba

TONY CROMBIE AND HIS ROCKETS

ROCK YOU SINNERS (1957)

UK - Black & White

Songs: Brighton Rock / Let You and I Rock

CROSBY, STILLS AND NASH

WOODSTOCK (1970)

USA - Colour

Songs: Suite: Judy Blue Eyes

NOTE: Woodstock was filmed in 1969.

ALAN DALE

DON'T KNOCK THE ROCK (1956)

USA - Black & White

Songs: I Cry More / Don't Knock The Rock

DICK DALE

BEACH PARTY (1963)

[UK: BEACH PARTY, U.S.A.]

USA - Colour

Songs: Swingin' and A-Surfin' / Secret Surfin' Spot

A SWINGIN' AFFAIR (1963)

USA - Black & White

Songs: Miserlou / A Swingin' Affair + 1 other song

MUSCLE BEACH PARTY (1964)

USA - Colour

Songs: Muscle Beach Party / Muscle Bustle [with Donna Loren] / My First Love

JIM DALE

SIX-FIVE SPECIAL (1958)

UK - Black & White

Songs: The Train Kept A-Rollin'

DANNY AND THE JUNIORS

LET'S ROCK (1958)

[UK: KEEP IT COOL]

USA - Black & White

Songs: At The Hop

VIC DANA

DON'T KNOCK THE TWIST (1962)

USA - Black & White

Songs: Little Altar Boy

BOBBY DARIN

PEPE (1960)

USA - Colour

Songs: That's How It Went, All Right

COME SEPTEMBER (1961)

USA - Colour

Songs: Come September / Multiplication

STATE FAIR (1962)

USA - Colour

Songs: A Grand Night For Singing [with Ann-Margret and Pat Boone] / This Isn't Heaven

JAMES DARREN

GIDGET (1959)

USA - Colour

Songs: Gidget / The Next Best Thing To Love

THE GENE KRUPA STORY (1959)

USA - Black & White

Songs: Let There Be Love

BECAUSE THEY'RE YOUNG (1960)

USA - Black & White

Songs: Because They're Young

GIDGET GOES HAWAIIAN (1961)

USA - Colour

Songs: Gidget Goes Hawaiian / Wild About The Girl

GIDGET GOES TO ROME (1963)

USA - Colour

Songs: Gegetta / Big Italian Moon

ALAN DAVID

GONKS GO BEAT (1965)

UK - Colour

Songs: Love Is A Dream

BILLIE DAVIS

POP GEAR (1965)

[USA: GO GO MANIA]

UK - Colour

Songs: Whatcha' Gonna Do

THE SPENCER DAVIS GROUP

POP GEAR (1965)

[USA: GO GO MANIA]

UK - Colour

Songs: My Babe

THE GHOST GOES GEAR (1966)

UK - Colour

Songs: When I Come Home / The Midnight Special / On The Green Light / Nobody Knows You When You're Down and Out / Instrumental

HERE WE GO ROUND THE MULLBERRY BUSH (1968)

UK - Colour

Songs: Every Little Thing / Looking Back

ALAN DAVISON

IT'S ALL OVER TOWN (1964)

UK - Colour

Songs: Please Let It Happen To Me

JOEY DEE AND THE STARLIGHTERS

HEY, LET'S TWIST! (1961)

USA - Black & White

Songs: Hey Let's Twist / Peppermint Twist / Round and Round / Roly Poly / Let Me Teach You How To Twist / Shout

TWO TICKETS TO PARIS (1962)

USA - Black & White

Songs: C'est Si Bon / What Kind Of Love Is This

<u>KIKI DEE</u>

DATELINE DIAMONDS (1965)

UK - Black & White

Songs: Small Town

CAROL DEENE

IT'S ALL HAPPENING (1963)

[USA: THE DREAM MAKER]

UK - Colour

Songs: The Boys On The Beach

THE DEL-VIKINGS

THE BIG BEAT (1958)

USA - Colour

Songs: Can't Wait

TERRY DENE

THE GOLDEN DISC (1958)

[USA: THE INBETWEEN AGE]

UK - Black & White

Songs: C'min and Be Loved / Charm / Candy Floss / The Golden Age

JACKIE DENNIS

SIX-FIVE SPECIAL (1958)

UK - Black & White

Songs: La Dee Dah

KARL DENVER

JUST FOR FUN (1963)

UK - Black & White

Songs: Can You Forgive Me

JACKIE DeSHANNON

SURF PARTY (1964)

USA - Black & White

Songs: Never Coming Back [with Patricia Morrow and Lory Patrick] / Glory Wave

C'MON, LET'S LIVE A LITTLE (1967)

USA - Colour

Songs: Baker Man / For Granted / Back-Talk [with Bobby Vee]

THE DIAMONDS

THE BIG BEAT (1958)

USA - Colour

Songs: Where Mary Go / Little Darlin'

DICK AND DEE DEE

WILD WILD WINTER (1966)

USA - Colour

Songs: Heartbeats

BO DIDDLEY

THE BIG T.N.T. SHOW (1966)

USA - Black & White

Songs: Hey Bo Diddley / Bo Diddley

THE LEGEND OF BO DIDDLEY (1966)

USA - Black & White

Songs: We're Gonna Get Married / Hey, Go Go

SWEET TORONTO (1971)

USA - Colour

Songs: Bo Diddley

NOTE: The Big T.N.T. Show was filmed in 1965. Sweet Toronto was filmed in 1969, and was reissued in extended form as 'Keep On Rockin'' in 1972

Later Movies: Let The Good Times Roll (1973), The London Rock & Roll Show (1973)

DION

TEENAGE MILLIONAIRE (1961)

USA - Black & White

Songs: Somebody Nobody Wants / Kissin' Game

TWIST AROUND THE CLOCK (1961)

USA - Black & White

Songs: The Wanderer / Run Around Sue / The Majestic

FATS DOMINO

SHAKE, RATTLE & ROCK! (1956)

USA - Black & White

Songs: Honeychile / Ain't That A Shame / I'm In Love Again

THE GIRL CAN'T HELP IT (1956)

USA - Colour

Songs: Blue Monday

JAMBOREE! (1957)

[UK: DISC JOCKEY JAMBOREE]

USA - Black & White

Songs: Wait and See

THE BIG BEAT (1958)

USA - Colour

Songs: The Big Beat / I'm Walkin'

Later Movies: Let The Good Times Roll (1973)

LONNIE DONEGAN

SIX-FIVE SPECIAL (1958)

UK - Black & White

Songs: The Grand Coolee Dam / Jack O'Diamonds

DONOVAN

THE BIG T.N.T. SHOW (1966)

USA - Black & White

Songs: Universal Soldier / The Summer Day Reflection Song / Bert's Blues / Sweet Joy

FESTIVAL (1967)

USA - Black & White

Songs: The War Drags On / Ballad Of A Crystal Man (Vietnam, Your Latest Game) / Colours [with Joan Baez]

DONT LOOK BACK (1967)

USA - Black & White

Songs: To Sing For You

WEAR YOUR LOVE LIKE HEAVEN (1967)

UK - Black & White

Songs: Three King Fishers / Oh Gosh / Wear Your Love Like Heaven / Ferris Wheel

IF IT'S TUESDAY, THIS MUST BE BELGIUM (1969)

USA - Colour

Songs: Lord Of The Reedy River

NOTE: The Big T.N.T. Show, Festival and Dont Look Back were filmed in 1965.

MAMIE VAN DOREN

UNTAMED YOUTH (1957)

USA - Black & White

Songs: Rolling Stone / Oo Bala Baby / Salamander / Go, Go, Calypso

TEACHER'S PET (1958)

USA - Black & White

Songs: The Girl Who Invented Rock and Roll

BORN RECKLESS (1958)

USA - Black & White

Songs: Home Type Girl / Something To Dream About / A Little Longer / Separate The Men From The Boys

THE BEAUTIFUL LEGS OF SABRINA (1958)

[ITALY: LE BELLISSIME GAMBE DI SABRINA]

Italy - Black & White

Songs: Don't Fool Around Sabrina

GUNS, GIRLS AND GANGSTERS (1959)

USA - Black & White

Songs: Anything Your Heart Desires / Meet Me Half Way, Baby

GIRL'S TOWN (1959)

USA - Black & White

Songs: Girl's Town / Hey Mama

SEX KITTENS GO TO COLLEGE (1960)

USA - Black & White

Songs: Baby

FREDDY UND DAS LIED DER PRÄRIE (1964)

[USA: FREDDY IN THE WILD WEST + THE SHERIFF WAS A LADY]

Germany - Colour

Songs: I'm Here To Stay

3 NUTS IN SEARCH OF A BOLT (1964)

USA - Colour

Songs: I Used To Be A Stripper Down On Main - Now I'm The Main Attraction On The Strip

LAS VEGAS HILLBILLYS (1966)

USA - Colour

Songs: Fresh Out Of Lovin' / Baby, Sweet Sweet Baby

ANGELA DOUGLAS

SOME PEOPLE (1962)

UK - Colour

Songs: Some People / Yes You Did / Too Late

CRAIG DOUGLAS

CLIMB UP THE WALL (1960)

UK - Black & White

Songs: Miss In-Between / Of Love

IT'S TRAD DAD! (1962)

[USA: RING-A-DING RHYTHM!]

UK - Black & White

Songs: Rainbows / Ring-A-Ding [with Helen Shapiro and Sounds Incorporated]

THE PAINTED SMILE (1962)

[USA: MURDER CAN BE DEADLY]

UK - Black & White

Songs: Another You / Painted Smile

THE DOVELLS

DON'T KNOCK THE TWIST (1962)

USA - Black & White

Songs: Do The New Continental / Bristol Stomp

BOB DYLAN

FESTIVAL (1967)

USA - Black & White

Songs: Mr. Tambourine Man / All I Really Want To Do / Maggie's Farm

DONT LOOK BACK (1967)

USA - Black & White

Songs: Subterranean Homesick Blues / All I Really Want To Do / Maggie's Farm / Only A Pawn In Their Game / The Times They Are A-Changin' / To Ramona / The Lonesome Death Of Hattie Carroll / Don't Think Twice, It's Alright / It's All Over Now, Baby Blue / Talking World War III Blues / It's Alright, Ma (I'm Only Bleeding) / Gates Of Eden / Love Minus Zero/No Limit

NOTE: Festival and Dont Look Back were taped in 1965.

Later Movies: The Concert For Bangladesh (1972), The Last Waltz (1978), Renaldo and Clara (1978)

DUANE EDDY

BECAUSE THEY'RE YOUNG (1960)

USA - Black & White

Songs: Shazam!

ELAINE AND DEREK

GONKS GO BEAT (1965)

UK - Colour

Songs: Broken Pieces

THE ENEMIES

RIOT ON SUNSET STRIP (1967)

USA - Colour

Songs: Jolene

LINDA EVANS

BEACH BLANKET BINGO (1965)

USA - Colour

Songs: He's My New Love [with The Hondells] / He's My Fly Boy [with The Hondells]

FABIAN

HOUND-DOG MAN (1959)

USA - Colour

Songs: Hound-Dog Man / I'm Growing Up [with Dennis Holmes while Stuart Whitman] / Single [with Stuart Whitman and Dennis Holmes] / This Friendly World / Pretty Little Girl / Got The Feeling

NORTH TO ALASKA (1960)

USA - Colour

Songs: If You Knew

MR. HOBBS TAKES A VACATION (1962)

USA - Colour

Songs: Cream Puff

SHELLEY FABARES

GIRL HAPPY (1965)

USA - Colour

Songs: Spring Fever [with Elvis Presley]

HOLD ON! (1966)

USA - Colour

Songs: Make Me Happy

ADAM FAITH

BEAT GIRL (1960)

[USA: WILD FOR KICKS]

UK - Black & White

Songs: I Did What You Told Me / Made You

MIX ME A PERSON (1962)

UK - Black & White

Songs: La Bamba

MARIANNE FAITHFULL

MADE IN U.S.A. (1966)

France - Colour

Songs: As Tears Go By

ANNA (1967)

France - Colour

Songs: Hier Ou Demani

SHANE FENTON

PLAY IT COOL (1962)

UK - Black & White

Songs: It's Gonna Take Magic [with Billy Fury]

IT'S ALL HAPPENING (1963)

[USA: THE DREAM MAKER]

UK - Colour

Songs: Somebody Else But Me

THE FIVE SATINS

SWEET BEAT (1959)

[USA: THE AMOROUS SEX]

UK - Black & White

Songs: In The Still Of The Night [Fred Pariss and The Satins]

Peter Checksfield

THE FIVE STARS

ROCK BABY - ROCK IT (1957)

USA - Black & White

Songs: Polly Molly / Your Love Is All I Need / Juanita

THE FLAMINGOS

ROCK ROCK ROCK! (1956)

USA - Black & White

Songs: Would I Be Crying

GO, JOHNNY, GO! (1959)

USA - Black & White

Songs: Jump Children

THE FLYING BURRITO BROTHERS

GIMME SHELTER (1970)

USA - Colour

Songs: Six Days On The Road

EDDIE FONTAINE

THE GIRL CAN'T HELP IT (1956)

USA - Colour

Songs: Cool It Baby

THE FOOL

WONDERWALL (1968)

UK - Colour

Songs: ?

THE FOUR COINS

JAMBOREE! (1957)

[UK: DISC JOCKEY JAMBOREE]

USA - Black & White

Songs: A Broken Promise

THE FOUR PENNIES

SWINGING UK (1964)

UK - Colour

Songs: Juliet / Running Scared

POP GEAR (1965)

[USA: GO GO MANIA]

UK - Colour

Songs: Juliet / Black Girl

<u>THE FOUR SEASONS</u>

BEACH BALL (1965)

USA - Colour

Songs: Dawn (Go Away)

THE FOURMOST

POP GEAR (1965)

[USA: GO GO MANIA]

UK - Colour

Songs: A Little Loving

FERRY CROSS THE MERSEY (1964)

UK - Black & White

Songs: I Love You Too

<u>GRAZINA FRAME</u>

WHAT A CRAZY WORLD (1963)

UK - Black & White

Songs: Bruvvers [with Joe Brown and Michael Goodman]

EVERY DAY'S A HOLIDAY (1964)

[USA: SEASIDE SWINGERS]

UK - Colour

Songs: A Boy Needs A Girl [with John Leyton] / Every Day's A Holiday [with John Leyton and Mike Sarne] / Second Time Shy / Say You Do [with John Leyton and Mike Sarne]

CONNIE FRANCIS

WHERE THE BOYS ARE (1960)

USA - Colour

Songs: Where The Boys Are / Turn On The Sunshine

FOLLOW THE BOYS (1960)

USA - Colour

Songs: Italian Lullabye / Follow the Boys / Waiting for Billy / Tonight's My Night / Sleepyland / Intrigue

LOOKING FOR LOVE (1964)

USA - Colour

Songs: Let's Have A Party / When The Clock Strikes Midnight / Looking For Love / Whoever You Are, I Love You / This Is My Happiest Moment / Be My Love / I Can't Believe That You're In Love With Me

WHEN THE BOYS MEET THE GIRLS (1965)

USA - Colour

Songs: But Not For Me [with Harve Presnell] / I Got Rhythm [with Harve Presnell] / Mail Call / When The Boys Meet The Girls

FREDDIE AND THE DREAMERS

WHAT A CRAZY WORLD (1963)

UK - Black & White

Songs: Camptown Races / Sally Ann

JUST FOR YOU (1964)

[USA: DISK-O-TEK HOLIDAY]

UK - Colour

Songs: You Were Made For Me / Just For You

EVERY DAY'S A HOLIDAY (1964)

[USA: SEASIDE SWINGERS]

UK - Colour

Songs: What's Cooking / Don't Do That To Me

OUT OF SIGHT (1966)

USA - Colour

Songs: Funny Over You / A Love Like You

CUCKOO PATROL (1967)

UK - Black & White

Songs: The Cuckoo Patrol / It Wasn't Me / Seems Like Things Are Turning Out Fine

NOTE: Cuckoo Patrol was filmed in 1965.

ALAN FREED AND HIS ROCK 'N' ROLL BAND

ROCK ROCK ROCK! (1956)

USA - Black & White

Songs: Rock 'n' Roll Boogie / Right Now

FREEDOM

NEROSUBIANCO (1969)

[UK: ATTRACTION]

Italy - Colour

Songs: ?

THE FUGS

CHAPPAQUA (1966)

USA/France - Black & White

Songs: ?

THE BOBBY FULLER FOUR

THE GHOST IN THE INVISIBLE BIKINI (1966)

USA - Colour

Songs: Swing A-Ma Thing / Make The Music Pretty

ANNETTE FUNICELLO

BEACH PARTY (1963)

[UK: BEACH PARTY, U.S.A.]

USA - Colour

Songs: Promise Me Anything (Give Me Love) / Treat Him Nicely

MUSCLE BEACH PARTY (1964)

USA - Colour

Songs: Surfer's Holiday [with Frankie Avalon] / A Girl Needs A Boy

BIKINI BEACH (1964)

USA - Colour

Songs: Because You're You [with Frankie Avalon] / This Time It's Love

PAJAMA PARTY (1964)

USA - Colour

Songs: It's That Kind Of Day / There Has To Be A Reason [with Tommy Kirk] / Pajama Party / Stuffed Animal

THE MONKEY'S UNCLE (1964)

USA - Colour

Songs: The Monkey's Uncle [with The Beach Boys]

BEACH BLANKET BINGO (1965)

USA - Colour

Songs: Beach Blanket Bingo [with Frankie Avalon] / I Think You Think [with Frankie Avalon] / I'll Never Change Him

HOW TO STUFF A WILD BIKINI (1965)

USA - Colour

Songs: Better Be Ready / The Perfect Boy / If It's Gonna Happen [with Frankie Avalon, Dwayne Hickman and Irene Tsu]

FIREBALL 500 (1966)

USA - Colour

Songs: Step Right Up

THUNDER ALLEY (1967)

USA - Colour

Songs: When You Get What You Want / What's A Girl To Do

HARVEY FUQUA

GO, JOHNNY, GO! (1959)

USA - Black & White

Songs: Don't Be Afraid Of Love [as 'Harvey']

BILLY FURY

PLAY IT COOL (1962)

UK - Black & White

Songs: Play It Cool / I Think You're Swell / Once Upon A Dream / Paint The Town / It's Going To Take Magic [with Shane Fenton] / Twist Kid / Play It Cool (reprise)

I'VE GOTTA HORSE (1965)

UK - Colour

Songs: I've Gotta Horse / Stand By Me / Do The Old Soft Shoe [with Sheila O'Neill] / I Like Animals (version #1) / Find Your Dream / Won't Somebody Tell Me Why / I Like Animals (version #2) / You Gotta Look Right For The Part [with Amanda Barrie, Jon Pertwee and Michael Medwin] / Grand Finale Medley: [with cast]

Later Movies: That'll Be The Day (1973)

THE GAMBLERS

I'VE GOTTA HORSE (1965)

UK - Colour

Songs: I Cried All Night

MARVIN GAYE

THE T.A.M.I. SHOW (1964)

[UK: TEEN AGE COMMAND PERFORMANCE]

USA - Black & White

Songs: Stubborn Kind Of Fellow / Pride and Joy / Can I Get A Witness / Hitch Hike

THE GENTRYS

IT'S A BIKINI WORLD (1967)

USA - Colour

Songs: Spread It On Thick

GERRY AND THE PACEMAKERS

THE T.A.M.I. SHOW (1964)

[UK: TEEN AGE COMMAND PERFORMANCE]

USA - Black & White

Songs: Maybelline / Don't Let The Sun Catch You Crying / It's Gonna Be Alright / How Do You Do It? / I Like It

FERRY CROSS THE MERSEY (1964)

UK - Black & White

Songs: It's Gonna Be Alright / Slow Down / Why Oh Why / Ferry Cross The Mersey / Fall In Love / This Thing Called Love / Think About Love / I'll Wait For You / Baby You're So Good To Me / It's Gonna Be Alright (reprise)

THE LORNE GIBSON TRIO

THE GHOST GOES GEAR (1966)

UK - Colour

Songs: Like Free [Lorne Gibson solo] / Listen To My Jingle Jangle / Meddlesome Matty

WAYNE GIBSON WITH THE DYNAMIC SOUNDS

IT'S ALL OVER TOWN (1964)

UK - Colour

Songs: Come On, Let's Go

ASTRUD GILBERTO AND STAN GETZ

GET YOURSELF A COLLEGE GIRL (1964)

[UK: THE SWINGING SET]

USA - Colour

Songs: The Girl From Ipanema

THE GOOFERS

BOP GIRL GOES CALYPSO (1957)

USA - Black & White

Songs: Wow

ROSCO GORDON AND THE RED TOPS

ROCK BABY - ROCK IT (1957)

USA - Black & White

Songs: Chicken In The Rough / Bopp It

LESLEY GORE

THE T.A.M.I. SHOW (1964)

[UK: TEEN AGE COMMAND PERFORMANCE]

USA - Black & White

Songs: Maybe I Know / You Don't Own Me / You Didn't Look Around / Hey Now / It's My Party / Judy's Turn To Cry

THE GIRLS ON THE BEACH (1965)

USA - Colour

Songs: Leave Me Alone / It's Gotta Be You / I Don't Want To Be A Loser

SKI PARTY (1965)

USA - Colour

Songs: Sunshine, Lollipops and Rainbows

CHARLIE GRACIE

JAMBOREE! (1957)

[UK: DISC JOCKEY JAMBOREE]

USA - Black & White

Songs: Cool Baby

LEE GRANT AND THE CAPITOLS

THE SORCERERS (1967)

USA - Colour

Songs: Sweet, Sweet Everything

THE GRATEFUL DEAD

PETULIA (1968)

USA - Colour

Songs: Viola Lee Blues

DOBIE GRAY

OUT OF SIGHT (1966)

USA - Colour

Songs: (Out Of Sight) Out On The Floor

JOHNNY B. GREAT

JUST FOR YOU (1964)

[USA: DISK-O-TEK HOLIDAY]

UK - Colour

Songs: If I Had A Hammer

JIMMY GRIFFIN

FOR THOSE WHO THINK YOUNG (1964)

USA - Colour

Songs: (I'm Gonna Walk All Over) This Land

ARLO GUTHRIE

ALICE'S RESTAURANT (1969)

USA - Colour

Songs: Pastures of Plenty [with Pete Seeger] / Car-Car Song [with Pete Seeger] / Alice's Restaurant Massacree

WOODSTOCK (1970)

USA - Colour

Songs: Coming Into Los Angeles

NOTE: Woodstock was filmed in 1969.

161

BILL HALEY AND HIS COMETS

ROCK AROUND THE CLOCK (1956)

USA - Black & White

Songs: Rock Around The Clock / See You Later Alligator / Rock-A-Beatin' Boogie / Happy Baby / Razzle Dazzle / R-O-C-K / Rudy's Rock / Rock Around The Clock (Reprise)

DON'T KNOCK THE ROCK (1956)

USA - Black & White

Songs: Don't Knock The Rock / Hot Dog Buddy Buddy / Calling All Comets / Goofin' Around / Rip It Up

HIER BIN ICH - HIER BLEIB' ICH (1959)

[UK: HERE I AM, HERE I STAY]

Germany - Colour

Songs: Viva La Rock & Roll [with Caterina Valente] / Hot Dog Buddy Buddy

BESITO A PAPA (1960)

Mexico - Black & White

Songs: Blue Suede Shoes / Crazy Man Crazy

JUVENTUD REBELDE (1961)

Mexico - Black & White

Songs: Shake Rattle and Roll / See You Later Alligator

Later Movies: Let The Good Times Roll (1973), The London Rock & Roll Show (1973), Blue Suede Shoes (1979)

ARCH HALL, JR.

WILD GUITAR (1962)

USA - Black & White

Songs: ?

ROY HAMILTON

LET'S ROCK (1958)

[UK: KEEP IT COOL]

USA - Black & White

Songs: Here Comes Love / The Secret Path To Love

HAWAIIAN BOY (1959)

Philippines - Colour

Songs: Unchained Melody / You'll Never Walk Alone + probably 1 other song

RUSS HAMILTON

SIX-FIVE SPECIAL (1958)

UK - Black & White

Songs: I Had A Dream

SOPHIE HARDY

THREE HATS FOR LISA (1965)

UK - Colour

Songs: I Fell In Love With An Englishman / A Man's World

JUDY HARRIET

BOP GIRL GOES CALYPSO (1957)

USA - Black & White

Songs: Hard Rock Candy Baby

SAY ONE FOR ME (1959)

USA - Colour

Songs: The Night Rock and Roll Died

JET HARRIS

JUST FOR FUN (1963)

UK - Black & White

Songs: The Man From Nowhere

JET HARRIS AND TONY MEEHAN

JUST FOR FUN (1963)

UK - Black & White

Songs: Hully Gully

WEE WILLIE HARRIS

MONDO DI NOTTE (1960)

[UK: WORLD BY NIGHT]

Italy - Colour

Songs: Don't Roll Those Bloodshot Eyes At Me / I Go Ape

TOTÒTRUFFA '62 (1961)

Italy - Black & White

Songs: Whole Lotta Shakin' Goin' On

RICHIE HAVENS

WOODSTOCK (1970)

USA - Colour

Songs: Handsome Jonny / Freedom (Motherless Child)

NOTE: Woodstock was filmed in 1969.

NORA HAYES

ROCK ALL NIGHT (1957)

USA - Black & White

Songs: Rock All Night / I Wanna Rock Now / Rock 'n' Roll Guitar

HEINZ

FAREWELL PERFORMANCE (1963)

UK - Black & White

Songs: Dreams Do Come True

LIVE IT UP! (1963)

[USA: SING AND SWING]

UK - Black & White

Songs: Live It Up / Don't You Understand

Later Movies: The London Rock & Roll Show (1973)

171

JIMI HENDRIX

MONTEREY POP (1968)

USA - Colour

Songs: Wild Thing [as The Jimi Hendrix Experience]

WOODSTOCK (1970)

USA - Colour

Songs: Voodoo Child (Slight Return) [Director's Cut only] / The Star-Spangled Banner / Purple Haze / Woodstock Improvisation [Director's Cut only] / Villanova Junction

NOTE: Monterey Pop was filmed in 1967 and Woodstock was filmed in 1969.

Later Movies: Jimi Plays Berkeley (1971), Rainbow Bridge (1972)

HERMAN'S HERMITS

POP GEAR (1965)

[USA: GO GO MANIA]

UK - Colour

Songs: I'm Into Something Good

WHEN THE BOYS MEET THE GIRLS (1965)

USA - Colour

Songs: Listen People / Biding My Time

HOLD ON! (1966)

USA - Colour

Songs: Hold On / A Must To Avoid / Where Were You When I Needed You / The George and The Dragon / Leaning On A Lamp Post / Got A Feeling / All The Things I Do For You Baby / Wild Love

MRS. BROWN, YOU'VE GOT A LOVELY DAUGHTER (1968)

UK - Colour

Songs: It's Nice To Be Out In The Morning / Holiday Inn / There's A Kind Of Hush / Lemon and Lime [with Stanley Holloway] / The Most Beautiful Thing In My Life / Instrumental / Mrs. Brown You've Got A Lovely Daughter

COLIN HICKS

EUROPA DI NOTTE (1959)

[UK: EUROPEAN NIGHTS]

Italy - Colour

Songs: The Book Of Love / Lea Lea / Twenty Flight Rock

VACANZE ALLA BAIA D'ARGENTO (1961)

Italy - Colour

Songs: Hollering and Screaming

THE HOLLIES

IT'S ALL OVER TOWN (1964)

UK - Colour

Songs: Now's The Time

UK SWINGS AGAIN (1964)

UK - Colour

Songs: Here I Go Again / Baby That's All

THE HONDELLS

BEACH BLANKET BINGO (1965)

USA - Colour

Songs: Cycle Set / He's My New Love [with Linda Evans] / He's My Fly Boy [with Linda Evans]

SKI PARTY (1965)

USA - Colour

Songs: Ski Party / The Gasser

BEACH BALL (1965)

USA - Colour

Songs: My Buddy Seat

THE HONEYCOMBS

POP GEAR (1965)

[USA: GO GO MANIA]

UK - Colour

Songs: Have I The Right / Eyes

DAVID HOUSTON

CARNIVAL ROCK (1957)

USA - Black & White

Songs: One and Only / Teen Age Frankie and Johnnie

CHRIS HOWARD AND THE THIRD WORLD

GIRL IN GOLD BOOTS (1968)

USA - Colour

Songs: Girl In Gold Boots

FRANK IFIELD

UP JUMPED A SWAGMAN (1965)

UK - Colour

Songs: Wild Rover / I Remember You / Once A Jolly Swagman / Look Don't Touch / Make It Soon / Botany Bay / I've Got A Hole In My Pocket / Lovin' On My Mind / I'll Never Feel This Way Again / I Guess / Cry Wolf / Waltzing Matilda

JACKIE AND GAYLE

WILD ON THE BEACH (1965)

USA - Black & White

Songs: Winter Nocturne

WILD WILD WINTER (1966)

USA - Colour

Songs: Snowball

JACKIE AND THE RAINDROPS

JUST FOR YOU (1964)

[USA: DISK-O-TEK HOLIDAY]

UK - Colour

Songs: The Loco-Motion

MICK JAGGER

PERFORMANCE (1970)

UK - Colour

Songs: Memo From Turner

NED KELLY (1970)

UK - Colour

Songs: Wild Colonial Boy

NOTE: Performance was filmed in 1968 and Ned Kelly was filmed in 1969.

Later Movies: Running Out Of Luck (1987)

JAN AND DEAN

THE T.A.M.I. SHOW (1964)

[UK: TEEN AGE COMMAND PERFORMANCE]

USA - Black & White

Songs: The Little Old Lady (from Pasadena) / Sidewalk Surfin'

JAN AND KELLY

IT'S ALL OVER TOWN (1964)

UK - Colour

Songs: The Trouble With Man [with Frankie Vaughan]

JAY AND THE AMERICANS

WILD WILD WINTER (1966)

USA - Colour

Songs: Two Of A Kind

THE JEFFERSON AIRPLANE

MONTEREY POP (1968)

USA - Colour

Songs: High Flying Bird / Today

WOODSTOCK (1970)

USA - Colour

Songs: Saturday Afternoon / Won't You Try / Uncle Sam's Blues [all songs are on the Director's Cut only]

GIMME SHELTER (1970)

USA - Colour

Songs: The Other Side Of This Life

ONE P.M. (1971)

USA - Colour

Songs: House At Pooneil Corner

NOTE: Monterey Pop was filmed in 1967, Woodstock in 1969, Gimme Shelter in 1969 and One P.M. in 1968.

MARV JOHNSON

TEENAGE MILLIONAIRE (1961)

USA - Black & White

Songs: Show Me / Oh Mary

PAUL JONES

PRIVILEGE (1967)

UK - Colour

Songs: Free Me / Free Me (Reprise)

JANIS JOPLIN

MONTEREY POP (1968)

USA - Colour

Songs: Ball and Chain [with Big Brother and The Holding Company]

PETULIA (1968)

USA - Colour

Songs: Roadblock [with Big Brother and The Holding Company]

WOODSTOCK (1970)

USA - Colour

Songs: Work Me, Lord [Director's Cut only]

NOTE: Monterey Pop was filmed in 1967 and Woodstock was filmed in 1969.

<u>KATCH 22</u>

BABY LOVE (1969)

UK - Black & White

Songs: Baby Love

<u>SUZIE KAYE</u>

C'MON, LET'S LIVE A LITTLE (1967)

USA - Colour

Songs: C'mon, Let's Live A Little

THE TERRY KENNEDY GROUP

THE GOLDEN DISC (1958)

[USA: THE INBETWEEN AGE]

UK - Black & White

Songs: Dynamo

KENNY AND THE WRANGLERS

BE MY GUEST (1965)

UK - Black & White

Songs: Somebody Help Me

THE KING BROTHERS

SIX-FIVE SPECIAL (1958)

UK - Black & White

Songs: Hand Me Down My Walking Cane / Six-Five Jive

THE KNICKERBOCKERS

OUT OF SIGHT (1966)

USA - Colour

Songs: It's Not Unusual

BUDDY KNOX

JAMBOREE! (1957)

[UK: DISC JOCKEY JAMBOREE]

USA - Black & White

Songs: Hula Love

BILLY J. KRAMER WITH THE DAKOTAS

THE T.A.M.I. SHOW (1964)

[UK: TEEN AGE COMMAND PERFORMANCE]

USA - Black & White

Songs: Little Children / Bad To Me / I'll Keep You Satisfied / From A Window

POP GEAR (1965)

[USA: GO GO MANIA]

UK - Colour

Songs: Little Children

THE LaDELL SISTERS

COUNTRY MUSIC HOLIDAY (1958)

USA - Black & White

Songs: Wang Dang Doo

THE LADYBIRDS

THE WILD, WILD WORLD OF JAYNE MANSFIELD (1968)

USA - Colour

Songs: ?

NOTE: This US group should not be confused with the UK vocal group of the same name, who tended to wear, erm, more "discreet" outfits!

DON LANG AND HIS FRANTIC FIVE

SIX-FIVE SPECIAL (1958)

UK - Black & White

Songs: Boy Meets Girl

JULIUS LaROSA

LET'S ROCK (1958)

[UK: KEEP IT COOL]

USA - Black & White

Songs: Crazy, Crazy Party / Two Perfect Strangers / Casual [with Phyllis Newman] / There Are Times

JACK LARSON

TEENAGE MILLIONAIRE (1961)

USA - Black & White

Songs: Back To School Blues

CAROLINE LEE AND JUDY JASON

JUST FOR YOU (1964)

[USA: DISK-O-TEK HOLIDAY]

UK - Colour

Songs: Teenage Valentino

JOHN LENNON

RAPE (FILM NO. 6) (1969)

UK - Colour

Songs: Everybody Had A Hard Year

SWEET TORONTO (1971)

USA - Colour

Songs: Blue Suede Shoes / Money / Dizzy Miss Lizzy / Yer Blues / Cold Turkey / Give Peace A Chance / Don't Worry, Kyoko (Mummy's Only Looking For Her Hand In The Snow) [vocals by Yoko Ono] / John, John (Let's Hope For Peace) [vocals by Yoko Ono]

NOTE: Sweet Toronto was filmed in 1969.

Later Movies: Imagine (1972)

KETTY LESTER

JUST FOR FUN (1963)

UK - Colour

Songs: A Warm Summer Day

GARY LEWIS AND THE PLAYBOYS

A SWINGIN' SUMMER (1965)

USA - Colour

Songs: Out To Lunch / Nitro

OUT OF SIGHT (1966)

UK - Colour

Songs: Malibu Run

JERRY LEE LEWIS

JAMBOREE! (1957)

[UK: DISC JOCKEY JAMBOREE]

USA - Black & White

Songs: Great Balls Of Fire

HIGH SCHOOL CONFIDENTIAL! (1958)

USA - Black & White

Songs: High School Confidential

BE MY GUEST (1965)

UK - Black & White

Songs: No-One But Me

SWEET TORONTO (1971)

USA - Colour

Songs: Hound Dog

NOTE: Sweet Toronto was filmed in 1969, and was reissued in extended form as 'Keep On Rockin'' in 1972.

Later Movies: The London Rock & Roll Show (1973), American Hot Wax (1978)

JOHN LEYTON

THE JOHN LEYTON TOUCH (1961)

UK - Black & White

Songs: Wild Wind / Son This Is She

IT'S TRAD DAD! (1962)

[USA: RING-A-DING RHYTHM!]

UK - Black & White

Songs: Lonely City

EVERY DAY'S A HOLIDAY (1964)

[USA: SEASIDE SWINGERS]

UK - Colour

Songs: All I Want Is You / A Boy Needs A Girl [with Grazina Frame] / Every Day's A Holiday [with Mike Sarne and Grazina Frame] / Say You Do [with Mike Sarne and Grazina Frame]

ABBEY LINCOLN

THE GIRL CAN'T HELP IT (1956)

USA - Colour

Songs: Spread The Word

THE LITTER

MEDIUM COOL (1969)

USA - Colour

Songs: (Under The Screaming Double) Eagle

LITTLE RICHARD

HOLLYWOOD SCREEN TEST (1956)

USA - Colour

Songs: Tutti Frutti / Long Tall Sally

DON'T KNOCK THE ROCK (1956)

USA - Black & White

Songs: Long Tall Sally / Tutti Frutti

THE GIRL CAN'T HELP IT (1956)

USA - Colour

Songs: The Girl Can't Help It / Ready Teddy / She's Got It

MISTER ROCK AND ROLL! (1957)

USA - Black & White

Songs: Lucille

CATALINA CAPER (1967)

USA - Colour

Songs: Scuba Party

SWEET TORONTO (1971)

USA - Colour

Songs: Lucille

NOTE: Sweet Toronto was filmed in 1969, and was reissued in extended form as 'Keep On Rockin'' in 1972.

Later Movies: Let The Good Times Roll (1973), The London Rock & Roll Show (1973), Down and Out In Beverly Hills (1985), The Pickle (1993)

JULIE LONDON

THE GIRL CAN'T HELP IT (1956)

USA - Colour

Songs: Cry Me A River

THE LONG AND THE SHORT

GONKS GO BEAT (1965)

UK - Colour

Songs: Love Is A Funny Thing

DONNA LOREN

MUSCLE BEACH PARTY (1964)

USA - Colour

Songs: Bustle [with Dick Dale]

BIKINI BEACH (1964)

USA - Colour

Songs: Love's A Secret Weapon

PAJAMA PARTY (1964)

USA - Colour

Songs: Among The Young

BEACH BLANKET BINGO (1965)

USA - Colour

Songs: It Only Hurts When I Cry

SERGEANT DEAD HEAD (1965)

USA - Colour

Songs: Two Timin' Angel

LOS BRAVOS

LOS CHICOS CON LAS CHICAS (1967)

Spain - Colour

Songs: Black Is Black / Don't Get In My Way / Going Nowhere / Sympathy / El Loco Soy Yo / Los Chicos Con Las Chicas

DAME UN POCO DE AMOOOR! (1968):

[UK: BRING A LITTLE LOVING]

Spain - Colour

Songs: Keeper Roots / Bring A Little Lovin' / Dime Donte E Stoy / Like Nobody Else / Make It Last

THE LOVIN' SPOONFUL

THE BIG T.N.T. SHOW (1966)

USA - Black & White

Songs: Do You Believe In Magic / You Didn't Have To Be So Nice

WHAT'S UP, TIGER LILY? (1966)

USA - Colour

Songs: The Fishin' Hole / Respoken

NOTE: The Big T.N.T. Show was filmed in 1965.

<u>LULU</u>

UK SWINGS AGAIN (1964)

UK - Colour

Songs: Shout

GONKS GO BEAT (1965)

UK - Colour

Songs: The Only One

TO SIR, WITH LOVE (1967)

UK - Colour

Songs: To Sir With Love [with The Mindbenders]

CUCUMBER CASTLE (1970)

UK - Colour

Songs: Mrs. Robinson / In The Morning Of My Life

NOTE: Cucumber Castle was filmed in 1969.

BOB LUMAN

CARNIVAL ROCK (1957)

USA - Black & White

Songs: This Is The Night / All Night Long

FRANKIE LYMON AND THE TEENAGERS

ROCK ROCK ROCK! (1956)

USA - Black & White

Songs: Baby Baby / I'm Not A Juvenile Delinquent

MISTER ROCK AND ROLL! (1957)

USA - Black & White

Songs: Love Put Me Out Of My Head / Fortunate Fellow

LOUIS LYMON AND THE TEENCHORDS

JAMBOREE! (1957)

[UK: DISC JOCKEY JAMBOREE]

USA - Black & White

Songs: Your Last Chance

KENNY LYNCH

JUST FOR FUN (1963)

UK - Black & White

Songs: Crazy Crazes / Monument

THE M6

THE GHOST GOES GEAR (1966)

UK - Colour

Songs: Seven Deadly Sins / The Place

GENE McDANIELS

IT'S TRAD DAD! (1962)

[USA: RING-A-DING RHYTHM!]

UK - Black & White

Songs: Another Tear Falls

CLYDE McPHATTER

MISTER ROCK AND ROLL! (1957)

USA - Black & White

Songs: Rock and Cry / You'll Be There

CINDY MALONE

WILD ON THE BEACH (1965)

USA - Black & White

Songs: Run Away From Him

THE MAMAS AND THE PAPAS

MONTEREY POP (1968)

USA - Colour

Songs: California Dreamin' / Got A Feelin'

NOTE: Monterey Pop was filmed in 1967.

JAYNE MANSFIELD

ILLEGAL (1955)

USA - Black & White

Songs: Too Marvellous For Words

THE GIRL CAN'T HELP IT (1956)

USA - Colour

Songs: Ev'ry Time (It Happens)

THE SHERIFF OF FRACTURED JAW (1958)

UK - Colour

Songs: Strolling Down The Lane With Bill / If The San Francisco Hills Could Only Talk / In The Valley Of Love

THE CHALLENGE (1960)

USA - Black & White

Songs: The Challenge Of Love

TOO HOT TO HANDLE (1960)

USA - Black & White

Songs: Too Hot To Handle / You Were Made For Me

HOMESICK FOR ST. PAUL (1963)

[Germany: HEIMWEH NACH ST. PAULI]

Germany - Colour

Songs: Wo Ist Der Mann / Snick-Snack Snuckelchen

PROMISES! PROMISES! (1963)

USA - Black & White

Songs: Lu-Lu-Lu I'm In Love / Promise Her Anything

LAS VEGAS HILLBILLYS (1966)

USA - Colour

Songs: That Makes It

NOTE: The songs in The Sheriff Of Fractured Jaw are sung by Connie Francis, with Jayne Mansfield miming to her voice.

THE MARCELS

TWIST AROUND THE CLOCK (1961)

USA - Black & White

Songs: Merry Twist-Mas

ANN-MARGRET

STATE FAIR (1962)

USA - Colour

Songs: Isn't It Kinda Fun [with David Street] / It's A Grand Night For Singing [with Ann-Margret and Pat Boone] / Willing and Eager [with Pat Boone]

BYE BYE BIRDIE (1963)

USA - Colour

Songs: Bye Bye Birdie / How Lovely To Be A Woman / One Boy [with Bobby Rydell]

VIVA LAS VEGAS (1964)

[UK: LOVE IN LAS VEGAS]

USA - Colour

Songs: The Lady Loves Me [with Elvis Presley] / Appreciation / My Rival

THE PLEASURE SEEKERS (1964)

USA - Colour

Songs: The Pleasure Seekers / Something To Think About / Everything Makes Music When You're In Love / Next Time

THE SWINGER (1966)

USA - Colour

Songs: The Swinger / I Wanna Be Loved / That Old Black Magic

Later Movies: Tommy (1975)

WINK MARTINDALE

LET'S ROCK (1958)

[UK: KEEP IT COOL]

USA - Black & White

Songs: All Love Broke Loose

TONI MARTINEZ

ROCK AROUND THE CLOCK (1956)

USA - Black & White

Songs: Sad and Lonely (Solo Y Triste) / Cueros (Skins) / Mambo Capri / Codfish and Potatoes (aka Bacalao Con Papa)

GLEN MASON

CLIMB UP THE WALL (1960)

UK - Black & White

Songs: What's Cooking Baby?

SUSAN MAUGHAN

WHAT A CRAZY WORLD (1963)

UK - Black & White

Songs: Alfred Hitchins / Please Give Me A Chance / I Feel The Same Way Too [with Joe Brown] / What a Crazy World We're Living In [with Joe Brown and Marty Wilde]

POP GEAR (1965)

[USA: GO GO MANIA]

UK - Colour

Songs: Make Him Mine

THE MELLO-KINGS

SWEET BEAT (1959)

[USA: THE AMOROUS SEX]

UK - Black & White

Songs: Tonite, Tonite

THE MERSEYBEATS

SWINGING UK (1964)

UK - Colour

Songs: Don't Turn Around / Fools Like Me

JUST FOR YOU (1964)

[USA: DISK-O-TEK HOLIDAY]

UK - Colour

Songs: The Milkman

THE MIGIL FIVE

SWINGING UK (1964)

UK - Colour

Songs: Mockingbird Hill / Long Tall Sally

KEN MILLER

I WAS A TEENAGE WEREWOLF (1957)

USA - Black & White

Songs: Eeny, Meeny, Miney, Mo

SURF PARTY (1964)

USA - Black & White

Songs: Pearly Shells

ROGER MILLER

THE BIG T.N.T. SHOW (1966)

USA - Black & White

Songs: Dang Me / Engine Engine #9 / King of the Road / England Swings

NOTE: The Big T.N.T. Show was filmed in 1965.

THE MINDBENDERS

TO SIR, WITH LOVE (1967)

UK - Colour

Songs: Instrumental / It's Getting Harder All The Time / To Sir With Love [with Lulu]

THE MIRACLES

THE T.A.M.I. SHOW (1964)

[UK: TEEN AGE COMMAND PERFORMANCE]

USA - Black & White

Songs: That's What Love Is Made Of / You've Really Got A Hold On Me / Mickey's Monkey

MARY ANN MOBLEY

GET YOURSELF A COLLEGE GIRL (1964)

[UK: THE SWINGING SET]

USA - Colour

Songs: Get Yourself A College Girl

MOBY GRAPE

THE SWEET RIDE (1969)

USA - Colour

Songs: Never Again

THE MODERN FOLK QUARTET

PALM SPRINGS WEEKEND (1963)

USA - Colour

Songs: Song Of The Ox Drivers

THE MOJOS

EVERY DAY'S A HOLIDAY (1964)

[USA: SEASIDE SWINGERS]

UK - Colour

Songs: Everything's Alright / Nobody But Me

THE MONKEES

HEAD (1968)

USA - Colour

Songs: Porpoise Song (Theme from Head) / Ditty Diego – War Chant / Circle Sky / Can You Dig It / As We Go Along / Daddy's Song / Long Title: Do I Have to Do This All Over Again?

THE MOONGLOWS

ROCK ROCK ROCK! (1956)

USA - Black & White

Songs: I Knew From The Start / Over and Over Again

MISTER ROCK AND ROLL! (1957)

USA - Black & White

Songs: Barcelona Rock

PATRICIA MORROW

SURF PARTY (1964)

USA - Black & White

Songs: Never Coming Back [with Jackie DeShannon and Lory Patrick] / That's What Love Is

JENNIFER MOSS

LIVE IT UP! (1963)

[USA: SING AND SWING]

UK - Black & White

Songs: Please Let It Happen

BILLY MYLES

SWEET BEAT (1959)

[USA: THE AMOROUS SEX]

UK - Black & White

Songs: The Joker

THE NASHVILLE TEENS

POP GEAR (1965)

[USA: GO GO MANIA]

UK - Colour

Songs: Tobacco Road / Google Eye

BE MY GUEST (1965)

UK - Black & White

Songs: Whatcha Gonna Do

GONKS GO BEAT (1965)

UK - Colour

Songs: Poor Boy

<u>**RICK NELSON**</u>

RIO BRAVO (1959)

USA - Colour

Songs: My Rifle, My Pony and Me [with Dean Martin] / Cindy [with Dean Martin with Walter Brennan]

THE WACKIEST SHIP IN THE ARMY (1960)

USA - Colour

Songs: Do You Know What It Means To Miss New Orleans

LOVE & KISSES (1965)

USA - Colour

Songs: Love and Kisses / Say You Love Me / Come Out Dancin'

SANDY NELSON

WILD ON THE BEACH (1965)

USA - Black & White

Songs: Drum Dance

ANTHONY NEWLEY

IDOL ON PARADE (1959)

UK - Black & White

Songs: Idle Rock-A-Boogie / Sat'day Night Rock-A-Boogie / I've Waited So Long / Idle on Parade / Won't Get No Promotion

JAZZ BOAT (1960)

UK - Black & White

Songs: Someone To Love

IN THE NICK (1960)

UK - Black & White

Songs: In The Nick / Must Be

LET'S GET MARRIED (1960)

UK - Black & White

Songs: Do You Mind / Let's Get Married / Confessions

THE NITESHADES

BE MY GUEST (1965)

UK - Black & White

Songs: Be My Guest

PATSY ANN NOBLE

LIVE IT UP! (1963)

[USA: SING AND SWING]

UK - Black & White

Songs: Accidents Will Happen

THE NOONEY RICKETT FOUR

PAJAMA PARTY (1964)

USA - Colour

Songs: Beach Ball

QUINN O'HARA

THE GHOST IN THE INVISIBLE BIKINI (1966)

USA - Colour

Songs: Don't Try To Fight It Baby

JOHNNY OLENN

THE GIRL CAN'T HELP IT (1956)

USA - Colour

Songs: My Idea Of Love / I Ain't Gonna Cry No More

ROY ORBISON

THE FASTEST GUITAR ALIVE (1967)

USA - Colour

Songs: The Fastest Guitar Alive / Pistolero / Good Time Party / River / Whirlwind / Medicine Man / Rollin' On / The Fastest Guitar Alive (Reprise)

Later Movies: Roadie (1980)

THE ORCHIDS

JUST FOR YOU (1964)

[USA: DISK-O-TEK HOLIDAY]

UK - Colour

Songs: Mr. Scrooge

JOHNNY OTIS

JUKE BOX RHYTHM (1959)

USA - Black & White

Songs: Willie and The Hand Jive

THE OUTLAWS

LIVE IT UP! (1963)

[USA: SING AND SWING]

UK - Black & White

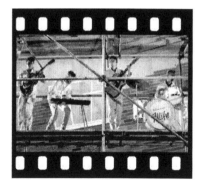

Songs: Law and Disorder

THE PARIS SISTERS

IT'S TRAD DAD! (1962)

[USA: RING-A-DING RHYTHM!]

UK - Black & White

Songs: What Am I To Do

CARL PERKINS

JAMBOREE! (1957)

[UK: DISC JOCKEY JAMBOREE]

USA - Black & White

Songs: Glad All Over

HAWAIIAN BOY (1959)

Philippines - Colour

Songs: Y-O-U / Where the Rio De Rosa Flows / That's All Right, Mama / Whole Lotta Shakin' Going On

PETER AND GORDON

JUST FOR YOU (1964)

[USA: DISK-O-TEK HOLIDAY]

UK - Colour

Songs: Leave Me Alone / Soft As The Dawn

POP GEAR (1965)

[USA: GO GO MANIA]

UK - Colour

Songs: A World Without Love

PETER, PAUL AND MARY

FESTIVAL (1967)

USA - Black & White

Songs: Come and Go With Me (Great Day in the Morning) / If I Had A Hammer

PINK FLOYD

TONITE LET'S ALL MAKE LOVE IN LONDON (1967)

UK - Black & White/Colour

Songs: Interstellar Overdrive

THE PLATTERS

ROCK AROUND THE CLOCK (1956)

USA - Black & White

Songs: Only You / The Great Pretender

THE GIRL CAN'T HELP IT (1956)

USA - Colour

Songs: You'll Never Never Know

ROCK ALL NIGHT (1957)

USA - Black & White

Songs: He's Mine / I'm Sorry

CARNIVAL ROCK (1957)

USA - Black & White

Songs: Remember When

GIRL'S TOWN (1959)

USA - Black & White

Songs: Wish It Were Me

EUROPA DI NOTTE (1959)

[UK: EUROPEAN NIGHTS]

Italy - Colour

Songs: You'll Never Never Know / My Dream

BRIAN POOLE AND THE TREMELOES

JUST FOR FUN (1963)

UK - Black & White

Songs: Keep On Dancing

SWINGING UK (1964)

UK - Colour

Songs: Do You Love Me

UK SWINGS AGAIN (1964)

UK - Colour

Songs: Someone, Someone

AFRICA SHAKES (1966)

South Africa - Black & White

Songs: Come On In

PREACHER SMITH AND THE DEACONS

ROCK BABY - ROCK IT (1957)

USA - Black & White

Songs: Roogie Doogie / Eat Your Heart Out

ELVIS PRESLEY

HOLLYWOOD SCREEN TEST (1956)

USA - Colour

Songs: Blue Suede Shoes

LOVE ME TENDER (1956)

USA - Black & White

Songs: We're Gonna Move / Love Me Tender / Let Me / Poor Boy

LOVING YOU (1957)

USA - Colour

Songs: Got A Lot O' Livin' To Do / Party / (Let Me Be Your) Teddy Bear / Hot Dog / Lonesome Cowboy / Mean Woman Blues

JAILHOUSE ROCK (1957)

USA - Black & White

Songs: Young and Beautiful / I Want to Be Free / Don't Leave Me Now / Treat Me Nice / Jailhouse Rock / (You're So Square) Baby I Don't Care

KING CREOLE (1958)

USA - Black & White

Songs: Crawfish [with Kitty White] / Steadfast, Loyal and True / Lover Doll / Trouble / Dixieland Rock / Young Dreams / New Orleans / King Creole / Don't Ask Me Why / As Long as I Have You

G.I. BLUES (1960)

USA - Colour

Songs: What's She Really Like / G.I. Blues / Doin' the Best I Can / Blue Suede Shoes / Frankfort Special / Shoppin' Around / Tonight Is So Right for Love / Wooden Heart / Pocketful of Rainbows / Big Boots / Didja' Ever

FLAMING STAR (1960)

USA - Colour

Songs: Flaming Star / A Cane and A High Starched Collar

WILD IN THE COUNTRY (1961)

USA - Colour

Songs: Wild In The Country / I Slipped, I Stumbled, I Fell / In My Way / Husky Dusky Day [with Hope Lange]

BLUE HAWAII (1961)

USA - Colour

Songs: Blue Hawaii / Almost Always True / Aloha 'Oe / No More / Can't Help Falling in Love / Rock-A-Hula Baby / Moonlight Swim / Ku-U-I-Po / Ito Eats / Slicin' Sand / Hawaiian Sunset / Beach Boy Blues / Island of Love (Kauai) / Hawaiian Wedding Song

FOLLOW THAT DREAM (1962)

USA - Colour

Songs: What A Wonderful Life / I'm Not the Marrying Kind / Sound Advice / On Top Of Old Smokey / Follow That Dream / Angel

KID GALAHAD (1962)

USA - Colour

Songs: King Of The Whole Wide World / This Is Living / Riding The Rainbow / Home Is Where The Heart Is / I Got Lucky / A Whistling Tune

GIRLS! GIRLS! GIRLS! (1962)

USA - Colour

Songs: Girls! Girls! Girls! / I Don't Wanna Be Tied / We'll Be Together / A Boy Like Me, A Girl Like You / Earth Boy / Return To Sender / Because Of Love / Thanks To The Rolling Sea / Song Of The Shrimp / The Walls Have Ears / We're Comin' In Loaded / Dainty Little Moonbeams

IT HAPPENED AT THE WORLD'S FAIR (1963)

USA - Colour

Songs: Beyond The Bend / Relax / Take Me To The Fair / They Remind Me Too Much Of You / One Broken Heart For Sale / I'm Falling In Love Tonight / Cotton Candy Land / World Of Our Own / How Would You Like To Be / Happy Ending

FUN IN ACAPULCO (1963)

USA - Colour

Songs: Fun In Acapulco / Vino, Dinero Y Amor / I Think I'm Gonna Like It Here / Mexico / El Toro / Marguerita / The Bullfighter Was A Lady / (There's) No Room To Rhumba In A Sports Car / Bossa Nova Baby / You Can't Say No In Acapulco / Guadalajara

KISSIN' COUSINS (1964)

USA - Colour

Songs: Kissin' Cousins (version #1) / Smokey Mountain Boy / There's Gold In The Mountains / One Boy, Two Little Girls / Catchin' On Fast / Tender Feeling / Barefoot Ballad / Once Is Enough / Kissin' Cousins (version #2)

VIVA LAS VEGAS (1964)

[UK: LOVE IN LAS VEGAS]

USA - Colour

Songs: Viva Las Vegas / Medley: The Yellow Rose Of Texas - The Eyes Of Texas / The Lady Loves Me [with Ann-Margret] / C'mon Everybody / Today, Tomorrow and Forever / What'd I Say / Santa Lucia / If You Think I Don't Need You / I Need Somebody To Lean On

ROUSTABOUT (1964)

USA - Colour

Songs: Roustabout / Poison Ivy League / Wheels On My Heels / It's A Wonderful World / It's Carnival Time / Carny Town / One Track Heart / Hard Knocks / Little Egypt / Big Love Big Heartache / There's A Brand New Day On The Horizon

GIRL HAPPY (1965)

USA - Colour

Songs: Girl Happy / Spring Fever [with Shelley Fabares] / Fort Lauderdale Chamber Of Commerce / Startin' Tonight / Wolf Call / Do Not Disturb / Cross My Heart and Hope To Die / The Meanest Girl In Town / Do The Clam / On A String / I've Got To Find My Baby

TICKLE ME (1965)

USA - Colour

Songs: (It's A) Long, Lonely Highway / It Feels So Right / (Such An) Easy Question / Dirty, Dirty Feeling / I'm Yours / Night Rider / I Feel That I've Known You Forever / Slowly But Surely

HARUM SCARUM (1965)

[UK: HAREM HOLIDAY]

USA - Colour

Songs: Harem Holiday / My Desert Serenade / Go East - Young Man / Mirage / Kismet / Shake That Tambourine / Hey Little Girl / Golden Coins / So Close, Yet So Far (From Paradise)

FRANKIE AND JOHNNY (1966)

USA - Colour

Songs: Come Along / Petunia, The Gardener's Daughter / Chesay / What Every Woman Lives For / Frankie and Johnny / Look Out, Broadway / Beginner's Luck / Medley: Down By The Riverside - When TSaints Go Marching In / Shout It Out / Hard Luck / Please Don't Stop Loving Me / Everybody Come Aboard

PARADISE HAWAIIAN STYLE (1966)

USA - Colour

Songs: Paradise, Hawaiian Style / Queenie Wahine's Papaya / Scratch My Back (Then I'll Scratch Yours) / Drums Of The Islands / A Dog's Life / Datin' / House Of Sand / Stop Where You Are / This Is My Heaven

SPINOUT (1966)

USA - Colour

Songs: Spinout / Stop, Look and Listen / Adam and Evil / All That I Am / Never Say / Am I Ready / Beach Shack / Smörgåsbord / I'll Be Back

EASY COME EASY GO (1967)

USA - Colour

Songs: Easy Come, Easy Go / The Love Machine / Yoga Is As Yoga Does / You Gotta Stop / Sing You Children / I'll Take Love

DOUBLE TROUBLE (1967)

USA - Colour

Songs: Double Trouble / Baby, If You'll Give Me All Of Your Love / Could I Fall in Love / Long Legged Girl (With the Short Dress On) / City by Night / Old MacDonald / I Love Only One Girl / There Is So Much World To See

CLAMBAKE (1967)

USA - Colour

Songs: Clambake / Who Needs Money / A House That Has Everything / Confidence / You Don't Know Me / Hey, Hey, Hey / The Girl I Never Loved / How Can You Lose What You Never Had

STAY AWAY, JOE (1968)

USA - Colour

Songs: Stay Away / Stay Away, Joe / Dominick / All I Needed Was The Rain

SPEEDWAY (1968)

USA - Colour

Songs: Speedway / Let Yourself Go / Your Time Hasn't Come Yet, Baby / He's Your Uncle, Not Your Dad / Who Are You (Who Am I?) / There Ain't Nothing Like A Song [with Nancy Sinatra]

LIVE A LITTLE, LOVE A LITTLE (1968)

USA - Colour

Songs: Wonderful World / Edge Of Reality / A Little Less Conversation / Almost in Love

CHARRO! (1969)

USA - Colour

Songs: Charro

THE TROUBLE WITH GIRLS (1969)

USA - Colour

Songs: Swing Down Sweet Chariot / The Whiffenpoof Song / Violet (Flower of NYU) / Clean Up Your Own Backyard / Signs Of The Zodiac / Almost

CHANGE OF HABIT (1969)

USA - Colour

Songs: Change Of Habit / Rubberneckin' / Have A Happy / Let Us Pray

NOTE: Charro features a song over the titles, with no on-screen performance.

Later Movies: That's The Way It Is (1970), Elvis On Tour (1972)

MIKE PRESTON

CLIMB UP THE WALL (1960)

UK - Black & White

Songs: Try Again

THE PRETTY THINGS

THE PRETTY THINGS - ON FILM (1966)

UK - Black & White

Songs: Midnight To Six Man / Can't Stand The Pain / Me Needing You / L.S.D.

WHAT'S GOOD FOR THE GOOSE (1969)

UK - Colour

Songs: Alexander / Eagle's Son / Blow Your Mind / It'll Never Be Me

Later Movies: Monster Club (1980)

PICCOLA PUPA

THE GHOST IN THE INVISIBLE BIKINI (1966)

USA - Colour

Songs: Stand Up and Fight

THE PYRAMIDS

BIKINI BEACH (1964)

USA - Colour

Songs: How About That [with Frankie Avalon] / Record Run

TOMMY QUICKLY AND THE REMO FOUR

POP GEAR (1965)

[USA: GO GO MANIA]

UK - Colour

Songs: Humpty Dumpty

THE QUICKSILVER MESSENGER SERVICE

REVOLUTION (1968)

USA - Colour

Songs: Codine

TEDDY RANDAZZO

ROCK ROCK ROCK! (1956)

USA - Black & White

Songs: The Things Your Heart Needs / Thanks To You / We're Gonna Rock Tonight [as part of The Three Chuckles] / Won't You Give Me A Chance

THE GIRL CAN'T HELP IT (1956)

USA - Colour

Songs: Cinnamon Sinner [as The Chuckles]

MISTER ROCK AND ROLL! (1957)

USA - Black & White

Songs: Kiddio / I Was The Last One To Know / Next Stop Paradise / I'd Stop
Anything I'm Doing / It's Simply Heaven

ANNITA RAY

SHAKE, RATTLE & ROCK! (1956)

USA - Black & White

Songs: Rockin' On Saturday Night

OTIS REDDING

MONTEREY POP (1968)

USA - Colour

Songs: Shake / I've Been Loving You Too Long

NOTE: Monterey Pop was filmed in 1967.

DELLA REESE

LET'S ROCK (1958)

[UK: KEEP IT COOL]

USA - Black & White

Songs: Lonelyville

CLIFF RICHARD

SERIOUS CHARGE (1959)

UK - Black & White

Songs: No Turning Back / Living Doll / Mad About You

EXPRESSO BONGO (1959)

UK - Black & White

Songs: Love / A Voice In The Wilderness / The Shrine On The Second Floor

THE YOUNG ONES (1961)

[USA: WONDERFUL TO BE YOUNG!]

UK - Colour

Songs: Nothing's Impossible [with Grazina Frame] / All For One [with cast] / Got A Funny Feeling / The Young Ones / What Do You Know We've Got A Show [with cast] / Friday Night [with cast] / Just Dance [with cast] / Lessons In Love [with Grazina Frame] / When The Girl In Your Arms Is The Girl In Your Heart / Medley [with cast] / We Say Yeah

SUMMER HOLIDAY (1963)

UK - Colour

Songs: Seven Days To A Holiday / Summer Holiday / Let Us Take You For A Ride / Stranger In Town / A Swingin' Affair [with Grazina Frame] / Really Waltzing / All At Once / Bachelor Boy / Dancing Shoes / The Next Time / Big News / Reprise

WONDERFUL LIFE (1964)

[USA: SWINGERS' PARADISE]

UK - Colour

Songs: Wonderful Life / A Girl In Every Port [with Melvyn Hayes and Richard O'Sullivan] / Home [with Melvyn Hayes and Richard O'Sullivan] / A Little Imagination / On The Beach / In The Stars [with Susan Hampshire] / We Love A Movie [with cast] / What've I Gotta Do / Do You Remember / All Kinds Of People [with cast] / A Matter Of Moments [with Una Stubbs, Melvyn Hayes and Richard O'Sullivan] / Youth and Experience [with cast]

FINDERS KEEPERS (1966)

UK - Colour

Songs: Finders Keepers / Time Drags By / Washerwoman / La La La Song / Oh Senorita / This Day / Paella

THUNDERBIRDS ARE GO! - TEST FILM (1966)

UK - Black & White

Songs: Shooting Star

THUNDERBIRDS ARE GO! (1966)

UK - Colour

Songs: Shooting Star

TWO A PENNY (1968)

UK - Colour

Songs: Two A Penny / Twist and Shout / I'll Love You Forever Today / Questions

Later Movies: Take Me High (1973)

THE RIGHTEOUS BROTHERS

BEACH BALL (1965)

USA - Colour

Songs: Baby What You Want Me To Do

A SWINGIN' SUMMER (1965)

USA - Colour

Songs: Justine

BILLY LEE RILEY

SPEED LOVERS (1968)

USA - Colour

Songs: Speed Lovers

THE RIP CHORDS

A SWINGIN' SUMMER (1965)

USA - Colour

Songs: Red Hot Roadster

<u>KIM ROBERTS</u>

LIVE IT UP! (1963)

[USA: SING AND SWING]

UK - Black & White

Songs: Loving Me This Way

ROCKY ROBERTS AND THE AIREDALES

THE WILD, WILD WORLD OF JAYNE MANSFIELD (1968)

USA - Colour

Songs: The Bird Is The Word

THE ROCKIN' BERRIES

POP GEAR (1965)

[USA: GO GO MANIA]

UK - Colour

Songs: He's In Town / What In The World's Come Over You

THE ROCKIN' RAMRODS

DISK-O-TEK HOLIDAY (1966)

[UK alternate edit: JUST FOR YOU]

UK/US - Colour

Songs: Play It

CLODAGH RODGERS

JUST FOR FUN (1963)

UK - Black & White

Songs: Sweet Boy

IT'S ALL OVER TOWN (1964)

UK - Colour

Songs: My Love Will Always Be There

NOTE: Clodagh Rodgers is billed as Cloda Rodgers in these two movies.

THE ROLLING STONES

THE T.A.M.I. SHOW (1964)

[UK: TEEN AGE COMMAND PERFORMANCE]

USA - Black & White

Songs: Around and Around / Off The Hook / Time Is On My Side / It's All Over Now / It's Alright / Let's Get Together [closing jam, with cast]

CHARLIE IS MY DARLING (1965)

UK - Black & White

Songs: The Last Time / It's Alright

ONE PLUS ONE: SYMPATHY FOR THE DEVIL (1968)

UK - Colour

Songs: Sympathy For The Devil

GIMME SHELTER (1970)

USA - Colour

Songs: Jumping Jack Flash / (I Can't Get No) Satisfaction / Love In Vain / Honky Tonk Women / Street Fighting Man / Sympathy For The Devil / Under My Thumb / Gimme Shelter

UMANO NON UMANO! (1972)

Italy - Colour

Songs: Street Fighting Man / Instrumental

NOTE: Gimme Shelter and Umano Non Umano were filmed in 1969.

Later Movies: Cocksucker Blues (1972), Ladies and Gentlemen The Rolling Stones (1974), Let's Spend The Night Together (1981), Live At The Max (1991), Shine A Light (2008)

THE RONETTES

THE BIG T.N.T. SHOW (1966)

USA - Black & White

Songs: Be My Baby / Shout

NOTE: The Big T.N.T. Show was filmed in 1965.

THE ROUTERS

SURF PARTY (1964)

USA - Black & White

Songs: Crack Up

THE ROYAL TEENS

LET'S ROCK (1958)

[UK: KEEP IT COOL]

USA - Black & White

Songs: Short Shorts

EARL ROYCE AND THE OLYMPICS

FERRY CROSS THE MERSEY (1964)

UK - Black & White

Songs: Shake A Tail Feather

BOBBY RYDELL

BYE BYE BIRDIE (1963)

USA - Colour

Songs: We Love You, Conrad [with Ann-Margret and Trudi Ames] / The Telephone Song [with Trudi Ames] / One Boy [with Ann-Margret] / A Lot of Living to Do [with Jesse Pearson, Ann-Margret and Lorene Yarnell Jansson] / Medley: (Everything Is) Rosie - (Everything Is) Hugo [with Janet Leigh, Dick Van Dyke and Ann-Margret]

ST. LOUIS UNION

THE GHOST GOES GEAR (1966)

UK - Colour

Songs: English Tea / I Got My Pride

SAM THE SHAM AND THE PHARAOHS

WHEN THE BOYS MEET THE GIRLS (1965)

USA - Colour

Songs: Monkey See, Monkey Do

JODIE SANDS

JAMBOREE! (1957)

[UK: DISC JOCKEY JAMBOREE]

USA - Black & White

Songs: Sayonara

TOMMY SANDS

SING BOY SING (1958)

USA - Black & White

Songs: Crazy 'Cause I Love You / Who, Baby, Who? / Soda Pop Pop / Sing, Boy, Sing

SANTANA

WOODSTOCK (1970)

USA - Colour

Songs: Soul Sacrifice

NOTE: Woodstock was filmed in 1969.

MIKE SARNE

EVERY DAY'S A HOLIDAY (1964)

[USA: SEASIDE SWINGERS]

UK - Colour

Songs: Crazy Horse Saloon / Love Me Please / Every Day's A Holiday [with John Leyton and Grazina Frame] / Indubitably Me / Say You Do [with John Leyton and Grazina Frame]

AL SAXON

JUST FOR YOU (1964)

[USA: DISK-O-TEK HOLIDAY]

UK - Colour

Songs: Mine All Mine

LINDA SCOTT

DON'T KNOCK THE TWIST (1962)

USA - Black & White

Songs: Yessirree

THE SEARCHERS

SATURDAY NIGHT OUT (1964)

UK - Black & White

Songs: Saturday Night Out / Saints and Searchers

JOHN SEBASTIAN

WOODSTOCK (1970)

USA - Colour

Songs: Younger Generation

NOTE: Woodstock was filmed in 1969.

THE SEEDS

PSYCH OUT (1967)

USA - Colour

Songs: Two Fingers Pointing At You

SHA NA NA

WOODSTOCK (1970)

USA - Colour

Songs: At The Hop

NOTE: Woodstock was filmed in 1969.

THE SHADOWS

THE YOUNG ONES (1961)

[USA: WONDERFUL TO BE YOUNG!]

UK - Colour

Songs: The Savage

SUMMER HOLIDAY (1963)

UK - Colour

Songs: Les Girls / Round and Round

RHYTHM & GREENS (1964)

UK - Colour

Songs: The Main Theme / Ranka Chank / The Drum Number / The Lute Number / Rhythm and Greens

FINDERS KEEPERS (1966)

UK - Colour

Songs: My Way / Spanish Music

THUNDERBIRDS ARE GO! (1966)

UK - Colour

Songs: Lady Penelope

DEL SHANNON

IT'S TRAD DAD! (1962)

[USA: RING-A-DING RHYTHM!]

UK - Black & White

Songs: You Never Talked About Me

HELEN SHAPIRO

IT'S TRAD DAD! (1962)

[USA: RING-A-DING RHYTHM!]

UK - Black & White

Songs: Let's Talk About Love / Sometime Yesterday / Ring-A-Ding [with Craig Douglas and Sounds Incorporated]

PLAY IT COOL (1962)

UK - Black & White

Songs: Cry My Heart Out / I Don't Care

A LITTLE OF WHAT YOU FANCY (1968)

UK - Colour

Songs: The Boy I Love Is Up In The Gallery / Don't Dilly Dally / The Lambeth Walk

DEE DEE SHARP

DON'T KNOCK THE TWIST (1962)

USA - Black & White

Songs: Slow Twistin' [with Chubby Checker]

DOUG SHELDON

JUST FOR YOU (1964)

[USA: DISK-O-TEK HOLIDAY]

UK - Colour

Songs: Night Time

SIMON AND GARFUNKEL

MONTEREY POP (1968)

USA - Colour

Songs: The 59th Street Bridge Song (Feelin' Groovy)

NOTE: Monterey Pop was filmed in 1967.

<u>NANCY SINATRA</u>

THE GHOST IN THE INVISIBLE BIKINI (1966)

USA - Colour

Songs: Geronimo

SPEEDWAY (1968)

USA - Colour

Songs: Your Groovy Self / There Ain't Nothing Like A Song [with Elvis Presley]

SLY AND THE FAMILY STONE

WOODSTOCK (1970)

USA - Colour

Songs: Dance To The Music / I Want To Take You Higher

NOTE: Woodstock was filmed in 1969.

JOAN SMALL

ROCK YOU SINNERS (1957)

UK - Black & White

Songs: You Can't Say I Love You (To A Rock 'n' Roll Tune)

MILLIE SMALL

SWINGING UK (1964)

UK - Colour

Songs: My Boy Lollipop / Oh Henry

JUST FOR YOU (1964)

[USA: DISK-O-TEK HOLIDAY]

UK - Colour

Songs: Sugar Dandy

THE SMALL FACES

DATELINE DIAMONDS (1965)

UK - Black & White

Songs: I've Got Mine

JIMMY SMITH AND HIS TRIO

GET YOURSELF A COLLEGE GIRL (1964)

[UK: THE SWINGING SET]

USA - Colour

Songs: Johnny Come On Home

DON SOLASH AND HIS ROCKIN' HORSES

ROCK YOU SINNERS (1957)

UK - Black & White

Songs: Rockin' The Blues

SONNY AND CHER

WILD ON THE BEACH (1965)

USA - Black & White

Songs: It's Gonna Rain

GOOD TIMES (1967)

USA - Colour

Songs: I Got You Babe / It's The Little Things / Good Times / Trust Me / Don't Talk To Strangers / Just A Name [last two songs are by Cher only]

SOUNDS INCORPORATED

IT'S TRAD DAD! (1962)

[USA: RING-A-DING RHYTHM!]

UK - Black & White

Songs: Ring-A-Ding [with Helen Shapiro and Craig Douglas]

LIVE IT UP! (1963)

[USA: SING AND SWING]

UK - Black & White

Songs: Keep Moving

JUST FOR FUN (1963)

UK - Black & White

Songs: Go

POP GEAR (1965)

[USA: GO GO MANIA]

UK - Colour

Songs: Rinky Dink / The William Tell Overture

VICKI SPENCER

TEENAGE MILLIONAIRE (1961)

USA - Black & White

Songs: Hello Mr. Dream / I Wait

TWIST AROUND THE CLOCK (1961)

USA - Black & White

Songs: Too Many Boyfriends / He's So Sweet

<u>SPIRIT</u>

THE MODEL SHOP (1969)

USA - Colour

Songs: ?

THE SPRINGFIELDS

JUST FOR FUN (1963)

UK - Black & White

Songs: Little Boat

IT'S ALL OVER TOWN (1964)

UK - Colour

Songs: Maracabamba / If I Was Down and Out

TERRY STAFFORD

WILD WHEELS (1969)

USA - Colour

Songs: Wine, Women and Song / Night Ride

THE STANDELLS

GET YOURSELF A COLLEGE GIRL (1964)

[UK: THE SWINGING SET]

USA - Colour

Songs: The Swim / Bony Moronie

RIOT ON SUNSET STRIP (1967)

USA - Colour

Songs: Riot On Sunset Strip / Get Away From Here

MARY STEELE

THE GOLDEN DISC (1958)

[USA: THE INBETWEEN AGE]

UK - Black & White

Songs: Before We Say Goodnight

TOMMY STEELE

KILL ME TOMORROW (1957)

UK - Black & White

Songs: Rebel Rock

THE TOMMY STEELE STORY (1957)

[USA: ROCK AROUND THE WORLD]

UK - Black & White

Songs: Take Me Back Baby / Butterfingers / I Like / A Handful Of Songs / Water, Water / You Gotta Go / Cannibal Pot / Will It Be You / Two Eyes / Build Up / Elevator Rock / Doomsday Rock / Teenage Party

THE DUKE WORE JEANS (1958)

UK - Black & White

Songs: It's All Happening / What Do You Do / My Family Tree / Happy Guitar / Hair-Down, Hoe-Down / Princess / Photograph [with June Laverick] / Thanks A Lot

TOMMY THE TOREADOR (1959)

UK - Colour

Songs: Medley: Take A Ride - Fiesta On Main Street / Singing Time / Tommy The Toreador / Where's The Birdie / The Little White Bull / Amanda

LIGHT UP THE SKY! (1960)

[USA: SKYWATCH]

UK - Black & White

Songs: Touch It Light [with Benny Hill]

IT'S ALL HAPPENING (1963)

[USA: THE DREAM MAKER]

UK - Colour

Songs: The Dream Maker / Maximum Plus [with Marion Ryan] / Egg and Chips / The Dream Maker (Reprise)

HALF A SIXPENCE (1967)

UK - Colour

Songs: All In The Cause Of Economy / Half A Sixpence [With Julia Foster] / Money To Burn [With Cyril Ritchard and Penelope Horner] / The Race / She's Too Far Above Me / Flash, Bang, Wallop / If The Rain's Got To Fall / I'm Not Talking To You [With Grover Dale] / This Is My World

THE HAPPIEST MILLIONAIRE (1967)

USA - Colour

Songs: Fortuosity / I'll Always Be Irish [with Fred MacMurray and Lesley Ann Warren] / Let's Have a Drink On It [with John Davidson]

FINIAN'S RAINBOW (1968)

USA - Colour

Songs: Something Sort of Grandish [with Petula Clark] / When I'm Not Near The Girl I Love / How Are Things in Glocca Morra? [with cast]

DODIE STEVENS

HOUND-DOG MAN (1959)

USA - Colour

Songs: What Big Boy?

SANDY STEWART

GO, JOHNNY, GO! (1959)

USA - Black & White

Songs: Playmates / Heavenly Father / Once Again [with Jimmy Clanton]

SONNY STEWART AND HIS SKIFFLE KINGS

THE GOLDEN DISC (1958)

[USA: THE INBETWEEN AGE]

UK - Black & White

Songs: Let Me Lie

THE STRAWBERRY ALARM CLOCK

PSYCH OUT (1967)

USA - Colour

Songs: The Storybook

THE SUPREMES

THE T.A.M.I. SHOW (1964)

[UK: TEEN AGE COMMAND PERFORMANCE]

USA - Black & White

Songs: When The Lovelight Starts Shining Through His Eyes / Run, Run, Run / Baby Love / Where Did Our Love Go

BEACH BALL (1965)

USA - Colour

Songs: Come To The Beach Ball With Me / Surfer Boy

<u>THE SWINGING BLUE JEANS</u>

UK SWINGS AGAIN (1964)

UK - Colour

Songs: Don't You Worry About Me / You're No Good

NEVILLE TAYLOR

CLIMB UP THE WALL (1960)

UK - Black & White

Songs: Medley [partially with Cherry Wainer]

TEN YEARS AFTER

WOODSTOCK (1970)

USA - Colour

Songs: I'm Going Home

NOTE: Woodstock was filmed in 1969.

THE 13TH COMMITTEE

WILD WHEELS (1969)

USA - Colour

Songs: I Hear Music / Makin' Love

THE THREE BELLS

THE GHOST GOES GEAR (1966)

UK - Colour

Songs: No-One Home

THREE OF AUGUST

WILD WHEELS (1969)

USA - Colour

Songs: A Thousand Butterflies / Merry Go Round

JOHNNY TILLOTSON

JUST FOR FUN (1963)

UK - Black & White

Songs: Judy, Judy, Judy

THE TITANS

BOP GIRL GOES CALYPSO (1957)

USA - Black & White

Songs: Rhythm In Blues / So Hard To Laugh, So Easy To Cry

THE TORNADOS

JUST FOR FUN (1963)

UK - Black & White

Songs: All The Stars In The Sky

FAREWELL PERFORMANCE (1963)

UK - Black & White

Songs: The Ice Cream Man

UK SWINGS AGAIN (1964)

UK - Colour

Songs: Blue, Blue, Blue Beat

THE TOYS

IT'S A BIKINI WORLD (1967)

USA - Colour

Songs: Attack

THE TRENIERS

THE GIRL CAN'T HELP IT (1956)

USA - Colour

Songs: Rockin' Is Our Business

DON'T KNOCK THE ROCK (1956)

USA - Black & White

Songs: Rockin' On Sunday Night

CALYPSO HEAT WAVE (1957)

USA - Black & White

Songs: Rock Joe / Day Old Bread and Cannede Beans

JUKE BOX RHYTHM (1959)

USA - Black & White

Songs: Get Out Of The Car

BIG JOE TURNER

SHAKE, RATTLE & ROCK! (1956)

USA - Black & White

Songs: Feelin' Happy / Lipstick, Powder and Paint

IKE AND TINA TURNER

THE BIG T.N.T. SHOW (1966)

USA - Black & White

Songs: Medley: Shake - A Fool In Love - It's Gonna Work Out Fine / Please Please Please / Goodbye, So Long

GIMME SHELTER (1970)

USA - Colour

Songs: I've Been Loving You Too Long

NOTE: The Big T.N.T. Show was filmed in 1965 and Gimme Shelter was filmed in 1969.

Later Movies: Tommy (1975) *[Tina Turner solo]*

THE TURTLES

OUT OF SIGHT (1966)

USA - Colour

Songs: She'll Come Back

CONWAY TWITTY

COLLEGE CONFIDENTIAL (1960)

USA - Black & White

Songs: College Confidential Ball

SEX KITTENS GO TO COLLEGE (1960)

USA - Black & White

Songs: Mamie's Song

THE TYRONES

LET'S ROCK (1958)

[UK: KEEP IT COOL]

USA - Black & White

Songs: Blast Off

THE VAGRANTS

DISK-O-TEK HOLIDAY (1966)

[UK alternate edit: JUST FOR YOU]

UK/US - Colour

Songs: Oh Those Eyes

RITCHIE VALENS

GO, JOHNNY, GO! (1959)

USA - Black & White

Songs: Ooh My Head

BOBBY VEE

SWINGIN' ALONG (1961)

USA - Colour

Songs: More Than I Can Say

PLAY IT COOL (1962)

UK - Black & White

Songs: At A Time Like This

JUST FOR FUN (1963)

UK - Black & White

Songs: (All You Gotta Do Is) Touch Me / The Night Has A Thousand Eyes

C'MON, LET'S LIVE A LITTLE (1967)

USA - Colour

Songs: What Fool This Mortal Be / Instant Girl / Over and Over / Back-Talk [with Jackie DeShannon]

THE VERNONS GIRLS

JUST FOR FUN (1963)

UK - Black & White

Songs: Just Another Girl

GENE VINCENT

THE GIRL CAN'T HELP IT (1956)

USA - Colour

Songs: Be-Bop-A-Lula

HOT ROD GANG (1958)

[UK: FURY UNLEASHED]

USA - Black & White

Songs: Dance In The Street / Baby Blue

IT'S TRAD DAD! (1962)

[USA: RING-A-DING RHYTHM!]

UK - Black & White

Songs: Space Ship To Mars

LIVE IT UP (1963)

[US: SING AND SWING]

UK - Black & White

Songs: Temptation Baby

BOBBY VINTON

SURF PARTY (1964)

UK - Black & White

Songs: If I Were An Artist

CHERRY WAINER AND DON STORER

CLIMB UP THE WALL (1960)

UK - Black & White

Songs: Medley [partially with Neville Taylor]

THE WALKER BROTHERS

BEACH BALL (1965)

USA - Colour

Songs: Doin' The Jerk

DEBORAH WALLEY

SKI PARTY (1965)

USA - Colour

Songs: Paintin' The Town [with Frankie Avalon, Dwayne Hickman and Yvonne Craig] / We'll Never Change Them

SERGEANT DEAD HEAD (1965)

USA - Colour

Songs: How Can You Tell / Let's Play Love [with Frankie Avalon]

THE WARRIORS

JUST FOR YOU (1964)

[USA: DISK-O-TEK HOLIDAY]

UK - Colour

Songs: Don't Make Me Blue

RAQUEL WELCH

A SWINGIN' SUMMER (1965)

USA - Colour

Songs: I'm Ready To Groove

THE WHACKERS

SWINGING UK (1964)

UK - Colour

Songs: Love Or Money

NANCY WHISKEY

THE TOMMY STEELE STORY (1957)

[USA: ROCK AROUND THE WORLD]

UK - Black & White

Songs: Freight Train [with The Chas McDevitt Skiffle Group]

THE GOLDEN DISC (1958)

[USA: THE INBETWEEN AGE]

UK - Black & White

Songs: Johnny O [with Sonny Stewart and His Skiffle Kings]

<u>SHEILA WHITE</u>

THE GHOST GOES GEAR (1966)

UK - Colour

Songs: I'm A Miss Fit / Switch Off The Night

THE WHO

MONTEREY POP (1968)

USA - Colour

Songs: My Generation

WOODSTOCK (1970)

USA - Colour

Songs: See Me, Feel Me / Summertime Blues

NOTE: Monterey Pop was filmed in 1967 and Woodstock was filmed in 1969.

Later Movies: Tommy (1975), The Kids Are Alright (1979)

THE WIGGLERS

BEACH BALL (1965)

USA - Colour

Songs: I Feel So Good / Surfin' Shindig / Wigglin' Like You Tickled / We've Got Money

MARTY WILDE

WHAT A CRAZY WORLD (1963)

UK - Black & White

Songs: A Lay-About's Lament / Oh What A Family [with Joe Brown] / Wasn't It A Handsome Punch-Up [with Joe Brown] / What a Crazy World We're Living In [with Joe Brown and Susan Maughan]

DANNY WILLIAMS

PLAY IT COOL (1962)

UK - Black & White

Songs: Who Can Say?

IT'S ALL HAPPENING (1963)

[USA: THE DREAM MAKER]

UK - Colour

Songs: A Day Without You

JACKIE WILSON

GO, JOHNNY, GO! (1959)

USA - Black & White

Songs: You Better Know It

TEENAGE MILLIONAIRE (1961)

USA - Black & White

Songs: The Way I Am / Lonely Life

STEVIE WONDER

MUSCLE BEACH PARTY (1964)

USA - Colour

Songs: Happy Street

BIKINI BEACH (1964)

USA - Colour

Songs: Happy Feelin' (Dance and Shout)

MARK WYNTER

JUST FOR FUN (1963)

UK - Black & White

Songs: Vote For Me / Happy With You / Just For Fun [with Cherry Roland]

JUST FOR YOU (1964)

[USA: DISK-O-TEK HOLIDAY]

UK - Colour

Songs: I Wish You Everything

THE YARDBIRDS

BLOW-UP (1966)

UK - Colour

Songs: Stroll On

THE ZEPHYRS

BE MY GUEST (1965)

UK - Black & White

Songs: She Laughed

PRIMITIVE LONDON (1965)

UK - Colour

Songs: Something About Her

<u>THE ZOMBIES</u>

BUNNY LAKE IS MISSING (1965)

UK - Black & White

Songs: Remember You / Just Out Of Reach

MOVIE INDEX

OTHER BOOKS BY PETER CHECKSFIELD

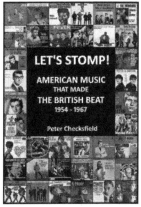 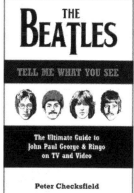 

 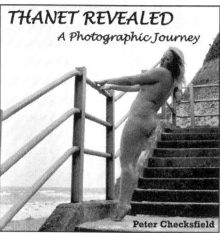

See www.peterchecksfield.com for more details!

ABOUT THE AUTHOR

An acknowledged expert in his field, Peter Checksfield is the author of 4 acclaimed books on music; 'Channelling The Beat!', 'Look Wot They Dun!', 'The Beatles – Tell Me What You See' and 'Let's Stomp', as well 'Thanet Revealed', a unique collection of nude photography. His books have been reviewed positively by 'Record Collector', 'Mojo', 'Shindig!', 'The Beat', 'Ugly Things', 'Folkrocks', 'Wired Up!', 'Making Time', 'The Joe Meek Society', 'The Daily Beatle' and more, and he has been interviewed by Spencer Leigh for his 'On The Beat' BBC Radio Merseyside show. He has also written for 'Record Collector', 'Now Dig This', 'Fire-Ball Mail' and 'The Beat'.

www.peterchecksfield.com

Printed in Great Britain
by Amazon